BITCOIN IN A NUTSHELL

THE DEFINITIVE GUIDE TO INTRODUCE YOU TO
THE WORLD OF BITCOIN, CRYPTOCURRENCIES,
TRADING AND MASTER IT COMPLETELY

SEBASTIAN ANDRES

WB PUBLISHING

CONTENTS

HOW TO USE THE BOOK

How to use the book

First of all I would like to thank you for your trust and for choosing me as your guide to embark on this journey into the world of Cryptocurrencies. This book will help you to understand and master this world with the objective of obtaining an excellent financial education through the comprehension and understanding of Cryptocurrencies. In this book we will go from the most basic to the most advanced.

We understand that entering the world of cryptocurrencies can be tedious and very slow because there is a lot of information that we must understand and assimilate, usually the pioneers in this type of technology are people who have no problem to generate passive income online because they have some basic knowledge of this world that can help them a lot. The purpose of this book is that you can also shorten this path and have the knowledge in time to take advantage of them, as you know the world of cryptocurrencies moves very quickly and you can not waste time.

This technology is here to stay and to give us, the ordinary people, more economic and financial freedom.

In my experience, one of the things that caught my attention when I became interested in cryptocurrencies back in 2011, was the concept of freedom that is related to currencies such as Bitcoin, Monero, Dash, Zcash, etc. where the control of the whole process always goes by hand with the user because of the privacy they provide. Don't worry, you will understand these concepts later on during the development of the book.

In this book I will teach you the different approaches to Cryptocurrencies and the technology behind it: starting from the actual concept of money to the Blockchain, why it works, what is the secret behind it and we will also debunk some myths related to some concepts.

The objective of this book is to teach you to have a more complete and complex notion about Cryptocurrencies, from the most basic concepts such as knowing how everything works, how the pieces fit together, to the most advanced.

I have also taken the time to suggest some resources to get you started on the right foot. Keep in mind that many of these links are affiliate links, so you will receive some discounts and benefits by using the referred link, at no cost to you. So take advantage of it.

I wrote this book not only to inform you about the world of cryptocurrencies but also to motivate you to take that step that is so hard for you and take action, that is why I want to ask you one thing, do not give up throughout this book, follow the advice at your own risk, I promise you that by finishing this book and applying step by step my advice and teachings you will be able to better understand this world and according to your personal actions achieve financial freedom or also support this initiative that gives power to us citizens against the current financial system that is too manipulated and makes a few people rich.

Again, thank you very much for purchasing this book, I hope you enjoy it.

ABOUT ME

Why should you listen to me?

Greetings, my name is Sebastian Andres, I am an entrepreneur, writer and world traveler. I am a cryptocurrency enthusiast since 2011 when I started to get interested in this world. I feel extremely blessed to have been born in this era, and to be able to experience the growth of these technologies such as the internet and cryptocurrencies.

For more than 10 years I have focused on developing several internet businesses, which taught me to develop my own strategies and methods to generate passive income. Cryptocurrencies was one of them and that is how I achieved financial freedom.

The purpose of my books, more specifically of the collection "Cryptocurrency Basics" (in which I bring the most current and reliable information on cryptocurrencies, if you are interested you can look for the other books in this collection, in which we address other cryptos) is to be a source of inspiration for you and generate a change in those who are not satisfied with the established and know that they can give more, that they can generate a positive change in their lives and get to design that lifestyle they want so much.

I am confident that this information will help you to get that final jump start and get into cryptocurrencies in depth.

DISCLAIMER

Important

Investing in financial markets such as cryptocurrencies and other assets can lead to money losses. The purpose of this book is only educational and does not represent an investment advice, for that there are already many professionals in the area that can help you. Proceed with caution, at your own risk and remember, never invest more than you are willing to lose.

By continuing to read this book you accept this Warning.

1

MONEY AND BITCOIN

The secrets of money

Money is that which forms a set of assets within a given cultural social activity: The economy, within which; people are totally convinced and willing to use it as a means or resource of payment to buy, acquire and sell goods, products and services.

The individual interprets and understands that money is that something that helps him and allows him to obtain what he needs, requires and desires, although it is clear that money is much more than a piece of trust and value capable of allowing negotiations at different levels and social, personal and business strata, among many others.

Money can be considered as any good or asset, widely accepted as a resource or means of payment by the characters and economic agents involved and participants in these exchanges or negotiations in the commercialization itself.

Money is that resource that, through its different presentations in currency, bills, cards, etc., continues to allow and facilitate the existence of the exchange of a resource for a good, the possibility of satisfying needs and solving requirements that demand to be delivered in exchange for receiving a payment for it. Money has also become a store of values that approves capitalization through savings, besides being an element of easy handling, transportation and storage, an important aspect.

As a GENERAL CONCEPT, money is the set of assets within an economy, regularly accepted by people willing to use it as a payment structure in the buying and selling process.

IF WE TALK a little more about money, let us add that it is immediately associated with printed paper bills and minted coins that are legal tender for the States and that in practice we are all willing to accept as a form of payment, convinced that it has a value through which purchases and sales are made, a material good that plays a role of interest in the daily life of society. We also handle it through debit cards (prepaid), credit cards and in some cases checks.

DEFINITIONS OF MONEY can be varied, diverse and far-reaching. In this sense, we could understand money as any element that those who make up a community or society are willing and in agreement to accept as a form of payment for goods, services or debts.

. . .

HOWEVER, we have all always been very familiar and related to bills and coins, cards and checks; also known as cash or legal tender, with which we can concretely buy or close a purchase or pay for something in exchange for a person or business, restaurant, store, transportation, etc. That is why the definition can also be narrowed to a more usual one, to say that money is a general good or asset openly accepted as a means or resource of payment that is used by a community.

HOWEVER, there is still another very important and attractive modality or type of money, and that is cash or money transfers, which people (customers) deposit in banks. Indeed, if the deposit made is directed to a checking account, the purchase could be paid directly and by means of personal checks (if applicable in the country) with a debit card, thus replacing cash with the convenience of keeping it stored in the financial entity.

THUS, coins and banknotes plus deposits made directly in banks are the elements that constitute and represent the most basic and elementary concept of money when it is understood as a means of payment.

MONEY, the legal means used by society to exchange a product or service. A material resource by means of which labor activities and workdays represented by work are also remunerated or compensated. A reference of measurement to carry out economic and financial transactions and operations.

Money facilitates the exchange of products and goods, represents the value of goods, and is regulated by the economic sectors of the regions to define the amount of money that should circulate in a country.

. . .

MANY COUNTRIES HAVE their own currency which represents the real purchasing power of the population, however, and in spite of this, at international level there are currencies such as the US dollar USD$, the pound £ and the euro €, currencies that are accepted for purchases or negotiations outside their legal tender zones or from where they originate almost everywhere in the world.

THE DOLLAR ALLOWS several countries in the world to make payments and acquire whatever they need to buy outside the United States, this fact is known as dollarization, and generally occurs in countries with weak currencies, also maintaining the circulation and use of its legal or own currency, with the idea of carrying and maintaining to have control over the issuance of money. Although also and for more positive reasons such as tourism, the euro, the pound and the US dollar are protagonists of commercial operations. Currently the Yuan is entering the market as a current currency.

AN INTERESTING EXAMPLE is the Euro €, a currency that by decree was introduced as official currency for II countries of the European Economic Community on January I, 1999, legally circulating in Germany, Austria, Belgium, Spain, Finland, Greece, Ireland, Italy, Luxembourg, Netherlands and Portugal; and that to date has managed to position itself as one of the most widely accepted currencies internationally.

FOR MOST COUNTRIES, paper money, on which banknotes or metals are printed to mint coins, and which circulates in a country, is closely related to a noble metal such as gold, which is its backing; however, global monetary and economic policies have changed and the backing it has today is through currencies, state or international securities, which is what favors inflation.

· · ·

How do we define money?

In accordance with the notion we have just seen of what money is in previous paragraphs, we can define it as any asset or good, widely and generally accepted in society as a means of payment and collection to carry out satisfactorily the transactions that can be carried out within a certain action or economic movement. We could also say that money is that element that has become practically indispensable for the daily life of human beings, since it fulfills functions that are usually irreplaceable by any other process or method known today.

It is also acceptable and valid to point out in a very simple, precise and quick way, that money is that material resource illustratively represented by bills, coins and others, which are used by individuals to comply with their payment commitments, and which their counterpart receives as an acceptable guarantee of the negotiation carried out, both being in agreement and in conformity with what has been paid and what has been delivered.

Money, from a tangible point of view, is an element that provides society with the facility to process commercial transactions in an expeditious, fast and reliable manner; it is a potential, capitalizing and representative resource; a personal and business support that is sustainable in base and value. An endorsement of importance in a wide range of acts of operational exchanges in the field of economic sciences.

In general economic-commercial lines and terms, it is worth noting in a very simple way that money is everything capable of being used by man and society, as a feasible means of exchange and settlement in exchange for products, services, goods or any other type of obligation or payment commitment.

As WE HAVE ALREADY SEEN, we find and have money in coin formats; as from its origins and as we will see below, in banknotes or paper money since the 19th century. Also electronic, something more current and that we will develop in detail, through documents and by means of cards or plastic money, all in favor of expediting commercial operations with a high degree of reliability, easy and effective to carry out. Money, an element that travels between hands, imposing a number value to that which is needed or desired to acquire.

MONEY THROUGH THE YEARS.

A BRIEF HISTORY of money up to the present day.

To BEGIN a fascinating historical journey on the origin and evolution of money, let us remember the great and important function it has in our society. Let us keep in mind that money is any asset accepted as a means of payment. Money, with all its variants and as we know it in modern times, arose due to the scarce effectiveness and dissatisfaction that barter, a practice initiated in the Neolithic era by the first human settlements, had been generating.

IN THE FIRST moments of human communities, there was practically no surplus or excess of the most valuable resource at that time: food. Our primitive inhabitants hunted exclusively to feed themselves, thus satisfying their immediate needs and keeping themselves energetic.

·   ·   ·

GIVEN the existential circumstances of the moment and the fact of guaranteeing life by providing their communities with the necessary food, at a date not precise for history; they began to store and conserve food in order to consume it in a programmed way without being damaged or lacking it. Their nomadic lifestyle made them move from one place to another in search of a suitable space for hunting, gathering, looking for food and better and better shelters.

THE REALLY PRESSING shortage arose in the Neolithic (10000 B.C. and 7000 B.C.), when the demographic level was increasing, a situation that forced the man of this era to develop and implement new and multiple means of sustenance for his people, giving rise to agriculture and livestock, being imperative the storage of large amounts of food for periods of scarcity.

ALSO, and as a natural balance, there were periods of good harvests; thus, the surpluses of these times were exchanged for other products from distant communities, thus giving rise to trade. To preserve these food goods, techniques such as salting, drying, curing and smoking were put into practice; depending on the geographical area, different strategies were used. In the African region, drying was used, in Northern Europe, smoking and in coastal areas, salting. Thus, merchandise campaigns were commercialized by means of exchange, paying with one product for the acquisition of another: barter.

WITH THE PASSING OF TIME, barter was also negatively affected as a commercial procedure. In this exchange it was necessary to locate, for example, a person interested in acquiring furs and that this in turn offered wine; or to establish an equitable value between a certain amount of wheat for wool. Barter did not have the power to establish a proportional cost in the products; for example, if a camel could have the same value as a cow or if meat and fish could be traded equally.

To provide an appropriate solution to this situation, the value of a product was established as a reference point, a product that was capable of being useful and regulating exchanges. For this purpose, cattle or wheat were used. These elements evolved according to market requirements, migrating to others that were easier to handle and move, such as gold, silver and bags of salt. Very punctually, salt was the favorite, even to fulfill a resulting function to make payments for the work done, thus giving rise to the word "salary". That which is received as a salary or payment for the execution of a specific work performed.

By MEANS OF BARTER, or exchange of a good, product or service in exchange for "something" that represented relative value, the first negotiations and ancient purchase and sale operations were carried out. As the years went by and the first inconveniences and difficulties with barter began to arise, a new alternative emerged: money and with it, the handling of the first coins; which represented an ideal, effective and timely solution for the moment.

The origin of money dates back to the 8th century and the use of the first coins in the 5th century. In the past, certain foodstuffs such as tea, cocoa and salt, cattle, fabrics and other representative and appropriate products were valuable resources to formalize negotiation, until the proposal to create currency by means of an alloy of silver and gold, measured and weighed to give proximity to the exchange, arose in Lydia, a region of Asia, by King Argos. This would replace payment with animals, food or other products. It should be noted that by the year 1000 B.C., China was already minting the first coins in bronze, gold and silver in the shape of swords and knives.

MANY EXHIBITS and stories about the first coins or banknotes that appeared there are told today, and all are equally respected and valued. In this regard it has been said and proven that the first coins appeared in Turkey, these were made of an alloy of gold and silver, these being the most valuable precious metals.

ALSO, Greece took as a tradition and custom to manufacture its own coins with the emblem of the locality that made them, the use of banknotes was implemented by the Mongol emperor Kublai Khan (28 SEP 1215-18 FEB 1294) who certified the amount of gold in existence before a bank. By the end of the 16th century and due to the great popularity of banknotes, banks began to produce them in large quantities as of 1694.

MONEY EMERGED and as such appeared in many areas of the world and in historically different times, this appearance not only responded to economic reasons but also to political, religious and social motivations and situations, such as buying a wife, paying dowry to the groom, presenting offerings to the gods or paying taxes to the government.

IT IS a propensity of humans to exchange things in order to meet shortages that have not been solved, in many communities have been taken from nature certain objects to be exchanged, the most common; rice, shells, limestone discs, metal discs and dog teeth, among many others.

THE FIRST COINS began to circulate in this way, becoming an essential part of commercial activity. As a result of this and its rapid expansion, Alexander the Great became the first to insert his image in the coins of the time, thus helping to expand this modality in the handling of money.

. . .

As TIME WENT BY, each measure of weight was assigned a name, thus giving rise to various denominations. An interesting example occurs with the following names: As and Roman Denarius, the latter is the one that gave origin to the word money. This is how, little by little, the concept and use of money was established and expanded throughout the world.

As WE HAVE SEEN, physical money, as it is known today, also had its changes and evolution, going from coins to paper money, represented by banknotes; a birth that occurred with the appearance of banking, but it would not be until the 19th century when metal coins would lose their supremacy. By then, the gold and silver format was abandoned to give way to other metals, and formal representations in banknotes formally appeared and circulated in a legal manner, guaranteed and backed by the State of the country, which gave its negotiations an amplitude in the holding and handling of money.

THERE WAS a standard within the monetary system that dominated since the 19th century, gold, by which the unit value of the currency was established based on a certain amount of this precious metal. In 1944, according to the agreements and resolutions of the monetary and financial conference of the United Nations, in Bretton Woods (Newpshire, United States), between July 1 and 22, the monetary system underwent an important change with the predominance of two major references and protagonists in the economy of the time: the dollar and gold.

THIS IS how the convertibility of the U.S. currency with gold was determined, being 35 dollars for 1 ounce of gold and the rest of the currencies according to the dollar. In 1971, Richard Nixon, President of the United States, declared the end of the gold standard, thus initiating the fluctuation of currencies.

. . .

THE SOCIO-ECONOMIC DYNAMICS of mankind has undergone important and constant changes throughout its existence, and this is how
alternatives continue to emerge that only seek to simplify the operations of exchanges and tangible payments for options, perhaps
abstract ones represented by Plastic Money and Electronic Money.

THE FIRST ONE, plastic money; conformed by a pattern represented by
groups of credit and debit cards or prepaid cards issued by the
banking system as substitutes for physical money, in cash. It owes its
name to the material from which the cards are made and manufactured. At present, they are widely used and accepted worldwide.

THE SECOND SAW the light of day in Japan in 2001 due to the large
amounts of physical money that would have to be handled for the
payment of public transportation, giving way to the creation of
rechargeable cards, and thanks to the transitions from paper money
to plastic and banking operations or services such as deposits and
bank transfers. Electronic money has been seen for some years as
responsible for the disappearance of physical money, otherwise it
would be an additional resource within the economic system as it is
currently known and managed.

SINCE THEN WE coexist with the use of different ways of handling
money by the different world economies, the well-known fiduciary
system, in which money does not have an intrinsic value, being
conditioned to the control and emission by the central bank of the
countries, as well as by other supranational corporations among
which we mention the European Central Bank for the communities
that constitute the Eurozone. Thus, money represented in paper,
coins or digital, does not currently have backing in precious metals,

its fiduciary value is based and rests strictly on the trust given by the individual, recognizing that it will be accepted as a secure means of payment by its participants.

If money did not enjoy this mutual trust and acceptance in society, the coins and bills that we use today in the negotiation of our commercial activity would be nothing more than simple paper tokens without any kind of value, except for the coins that, depending on the metal with which they were made, would have a value according to their weight.

NOWADAYS, societies have several and varied forms of payment such as checks, credit cards, prepaid cards and electronic transfers; they are used to facilitate the processes and procedures to obtain goods and services without having to transport or carry cash with them at all times. Debit or prepaid cards also facilitate payments in stores, stores and restaurants through points of sale and allow cash withdrawals through ATMs of the various interbank networks.

IT IS VERY possible that in the very near future and in the short term, thanks to the evolution of technology, money will already be electronic, which could be used anonymously from the Internet or in an operating center through a microchip.

FIAT MONEY AND INTRINSIC VALUE.

DEAR READER, probably before resuming this reading you made some purchase or perhaps organized your wallet, handled some money; some coins or bills. Now, you may have wondered at some point, what is really that money that you have on hand or is deposited in your bank account, do you know what kind of money it is, well, it is money known by the qualifier fiat, which, translated from Latin into English, means "let it be done" or "let it be so".

MONEY RECEIVES this name because it has been given by decree, order and imposition of the highest authority that governs or rules a country. That money that we handle daily, cannot at any time be exchanged for gold or silver, you can buy it, but not exchange it, since it has no value that allows such equity.

In our world there is only fiat money, and going back to recent history, it is worth noting that this turn of events began in 1971, when the United States broke the gold standard. You may wonder why this happened. From the governmental period of French President Charles de Gaulle (1959-1969) and until 1970 with Georges Pompidou as President, France exchanged all the dollars that circulated and existed in the country for gold from the U.S. Federal Reserve.

THIS GENERATED an extreme drop in the gold reserves of the United States and a loss of the influence exercised by the dollar abroad, since the nation gave up its gold and in exchange received its currency back. In addition to this strategy executed by France, the government of President Richard Nixon was heavily indebted as a result of the Vietnam War, and so on August 15, 1971, Nixon decided to repeal the convertibility of the dollar, closing the doors to the gold standard worldwide.

FROM THEN ON, the money in circulation ceased to have the backing and the treasured value given by the government that printed it, and went from fiduciary to fiat, money without tangible backing, simply money with value attributed by agreement. Despite all the above, historical facts, decrees and economic determinations of nations, money continues to move the world, even though it is fiat; but, why does money have value?

Simple and in a single word, the money we use every day enjoys "trust", because the paper money and metal that we use every day and practically all over the world is fiat currency and has no intrinsic value whatsoever.

DEFINED, we can say that the intrinsic value of money made up of paper money or fiat currency, is the conglomerate of the value represented by the essential elements that compose it: paper, ink and trust, indisputably. If there came a time when the individual lost total confidence in money, we would be left with only a representation printed on a piece of paper with ink with a value equal to zero.

WHAT ABOUT PHYSICAL CURRENCIES, unlike printed banknotes, coins do have an intrinsic value and this is represented by the weight of the metal with which they have been minted, however, these circulating physical currencies are so perishable compared to paper money, electronic or bank money, that their impact on the current banking system is practically irrelevant.

THIS REALLY MEANS that the euro, the dollar, the pound, the yen, etc., not being backed by something truly tangible like gold or silver, are simply nomenclatures of currencies printed on paper, which we all believe in out of conviction, giving them through trust a fiduciary value.

AMONG THE GREATEST setbacks and problems caused by the lack of intrinsic value in money, is to have the production of currency under total control, since not having an element that serves as an anchor, the tendency of this type of currency is inflationary.

. . .

LET us make clear then two important concepts on types of money that we have seen:

- **Fiduciary:** It is the one that is backed by the trust and faith placed in the money by society, it is not safeguarded or protected by precious metals or anything else that is the exclusive guarantee of payment by the issuing body. A fiat currency is a national currency that is not associated with the price of a globally traded commodity such as gold and silver.
- **Fiat:** It is the money by decree, differing from the previous one due to its governmental imposition granting it the character of legal tender and is used in large quantities by governments and international institutions as part of their international reserves, also using it as the reference currency to establish prices of goods traded at an international global level such as oil and gold among many others.
- **Some models of fiat currencies:** The U.S. dollar, the euro, the yen and other major reserve currencies such as the German mark, the pound sterling, the French franc and the Swiss franc.

THANKS TO MONEY, our needs, tastes, pleasures and negotiations can be satisfied; however, it is important to keep in mind that the money usually used has no intrinsic value, it is worth the trust we have in it. At the least thought moment and as it has been historically demonstrated, it will become a simple piece of paper. It will be convenient to have only the money that is necessary for current expenses, the rest should be invested in tangible goods.

LET us reinforce a little the basic concept of this section on fiat money, This type of money, which was already used in China in the eleventh century with the Ming Dynasty, is money that by itself has no value and neither enjoys nor is backed by reserves in precious metals such as gold or silver of its issuing financial institution, its value exists simply because it has been decreed as money and because the authorities, through its laws says that it is money and has that value.

WITH THE APPEARANCE of fiat money, these problems that we have exposed and that fiat money represents are corrected: the issuing financial entity or bank is no longer obliged to deliver gold or silver in exchange for its bills and coins, and the value of its currency no longer depends on the value of its gold, although it is still viable, in some way, to continue using gold in a similar way to the way money is used.

THIS IS the reason why most countries around the world adopted this system throughout the 20th century, becoming universal from the moment when the U.S. dollar abandoned the gold standard in 1971. Currently, there is no longer any such thing as fiat money; all the money we know and that circulates in the world is fiat money.

HOWEVER, the fact that fiat money is not backed by the country's gold reserves does not mean that it is not backed by anything. Although from the official and institutional point of view this money has value because the law says it is worth and so establishes; its value still depends on the trust and confidence that people place in it and continue to believe or trust in accepting it as a means of payment and their official legal tender.

IT IS safe to say that the backing of a modern currency is in the economy of the country that issues it. A country becomes rich and prosperous with a healthy economy, and thus it will be able to have a strong currency that will be well received and accepted with open hands in the market; otherwise, it will be impossible.

DIGITAL MONEY and how we got to it.

FIRST, let's share a brief and universal definition of what digital money is: A resource for commercial exchange electronically, not manually or physically; allowing immediate transactions and transfers regardless of distances or schedules, even specific type of currency.

SINCE VERY RECENT times there are also the already worldwide known virtual currencies, such as cryptocurrencies; a type of digital currency valid practically all over the world for all types of banking and commercial operations. From large corporations to personal level, we make purchases and pay with digital money, an abstract if the term fits; because in most cases we will only see a number reflected in the statement of account, without having a single one of these currencies at hand.

THE DIGITAL MONEY or also digital currency, virtual currency, virtual currency, virtual money or electronic money, knows no borders or geographical boundaries, nor is it subject to a centralized condition. This digital money has similar conditions and properties to physical currencies only because of its acceptance, operational availability and negotiation.

CURRENCIES AND CRYPTOCURRENCIES represent types of digital currencies and their conversion is incorrect. On a par with traditional money, these currencies are equally useful when acquiring goods, products or services, although they may be subject to restriction by some type of community, online services or social networks.

SOME DIGITAL CURRENCIES such as Bitcoin, are characterized by being decentralized currencies, since there is no intervention, control, supervisory body or neuralgic point that controls its issuance, supply or movement; its value is stored in an electronic support.

ELECTRONIC MONEY IS IMMERSED in any payment system or method that involves the use of resources through digital media. These include debit cards, credit cards and electronic purses, among many others. All these payment elements require the use of computerized software, as well as hardware in some cases and internet connection to carry out transactions.

We are referring to a specific concept of money expressed in bits (minimum unit of computerized information). It is a means of payment that lacks a physical unit, performing its operations through the exchange of bits, without the use of banknotes, coins, cards or any other conventional resource. Because of this, we will also find other types of denominations, such as e-money, cyber-currency or digital-cash.

THE NEW MARKET TRENDS, its demands, requirements and more expeditious solutions, formed an accumulation of variants that demanded to the diverse economies and monetary movements of the planet; a more universal, practical and valuable way; within reach of a click. Thanks to the growing technological innovations, operations are formalized at all levels under this format of money. Now, let's see a little more of history and how digital money has arrived or has arrived to us today.

· · ·

IN THE YEAR 1440 Johannes Gensfleisch zur Laden zum Gutenberg, better known as Johannes Gutenberg, invented the printing press and paradoxically all kinds of regulations for printing books appeared immediately, which constituted capital punishment in some countries. Why this reference?

The U.S. Constitution prohibits its citizens from issuing or minting their own currency and, in turn, competing with the U.S. dollar. However, in 1998 Bernard von NotHaus creates his own Liberty Dollar coin (ALD Free Dollar), available in gold, silver and platinum with a value greater than five cents and similar to it. On March 18, 2011, he is convicted of committing "domestic terrorism" and manufacturing counterfeit coins that would seek to undermine confidence in the traditional dollar.

VON NOTHAUS IS CURRENTLY under house arrest, awaiting a possible sentence that could be close to 20 years in prison, for the crime of making his own money.

YEARS LATER, AT A HACKERS' convention held in Holland, one of the participants, identified under the pseudonym of Satoshi Nakamoto, contacted Bernard von NotHaus and expressed his great admiration for such a feat, letting him know that he was his inspiration to create a new currency.

THERE IS much talk about what is the first digital currency, while in the banks of the world, and for years, digital money is constantly being created, which does not exist neither in gold, nor in paper, nor in coins; only in figures and numbers in a "digital" bank account.

LET'S DO AN EASY, realistic and practical mathematical exercise. When a saver makes a deposit of 1000 dollars in his bank account, the entity will keep part of his money and will lend the rest, however, in his account, the client will continue to have and count on his 1000 dollars, which in reality he does not have. This is a clear example that the bank has created and generated more than 900 digital dollars from a deposit for every 1000 dollars a saver makes. We buy and pay with abstract figures of a capital that only appears in digits.

To GIVE a clear example of how we arrived at digital money, let's go to the middle of the 20th century when the first credit card was created by Frank McNamara through Diner's Club. He took it for granted that paper money would become a different level of importance, and that in a few years, more than half of his customers and a very high number of North American inhabitants would have a credit card in their possession.

In 2009, the Dow suffered a sharp fall while Wall Street became a nightmare; a product of distrust in banking, governments and insecurity in centralized money. At that very moment, a white paper describing the Bitcoin protocol was published and, despite the fact that its creator is anonymous, many individuals gave their approval for it to proceed and be implemented.

So, among news, trends, requirements, needs, weaknesses and strengths of money in different formats; with its changing dynamics in all societies of the world, facing the weaknesses and opportunities in all its practices and requirements in the operation of the sale, purchase and payment; comes to our "hands" and our computers and mobile devices, around the technology of the moment, a valuable resource: digital money, reliable, safe, current and active for easy and immediate negotiation. A new way to move money and capitalize in some way or another.

. . .

As GUTENBERG, von NotHaus and many others, governments impose sanctions to all those who consider a universal risk with their creations in inventions; however, history is the one that finally is in charge of dictating final and determining sentence. The Gutenberg printing press remains and has become, five centuries later, one of the most revolutionary inventions in favor of humanity. 22 years after having seen his own currency created, NotHaus is condemned and put under arrest, while other entrepreneurs do the same taking this character as inspiration. So, a brief review of how digital money came about and how we got there.

LET us bear in mind that money is any asset or good universally admitted as a means of payment by economic actors and exchange participants valid for their negotiations, fulfilling a basic and fundamental function as a unit of account and store of value. There are several types and formats of money handling it, namely and remember; coins, banknotes, debit cards, credit cards, electronic movements, cryptocurrencies, digital currencies among many others.

THE MONEY WE KNOW, the one we have in our wallets, that we use every day, that we take to the bank and that is represented by bills and coins, needs to be duly endorsed and certified by the issuing bank. The legitimacy of the currency and trust in it, must be its construction mechanism for its agreed acceptance.

TODAY, governments have the autonomy and power, through the establishment of their laws, to decree which will be the specimen of money established for its legal tender, while other entities such as central banks and mints, will be responsible for the responsibility and commitment to regulate and inspect the monetary policy of their own economy, as well as the creation of coins and bills according to their needs to ensure and satisfy their community in their demands for cash-circulating physical money.

Looking at the panorama from the point of view of the social and economic sciences, the socio-cultural element or factor is immersed in the game, since having a currency as a public good issued by its government, and given that it (money) provides a service of common predominance; it must be regulated by the competent authorities of the nation's public sector, as has been said, through the central banks and mints. A strategy that will avoid the creation of other currencies or parallel circulating currency by third parties, which would put at risk the one endorsed as legal tender.

WE CONCLUDE this interesting section on money with an excellent phrase of the English statesman Benjamin Disraeli (1804-1881), who once said:

"THE BEST THING we can do for another is not only to share with him our riches, but to show him his."

RECOGNIZE YOUR TALENTS, enjoy your riches and be happy to see the other also with his.

2

BLOCKCHAIN, BITCOIN AND THE ORIGIN OF CRYPTOCURRENCIES

Cryptography and Digital Cash

Man has always been in the need to protect, reserve and hide some kind of information or data, and not just from the computer age, computers, internet or mobile devices; we have always jealously guarded that which in due course only we will disclose if necessary.

The meaning of the word cryptography, translates to a generic term that describes those techniques that allow in some way to encrypt or abbreviate messages, data and information to make them unintelligible, without the need to resort to certain or certain specific actions. There are two expressions or verbs directly associated with cryptography: encrypt and encrypt, which are very frequently used.

Cryptography is based on and totally immersed in arithmetic. Let's look at the case of encrypting or ciphering a text. In this process, the letters that make up the message are converted into a series or set of numbers in the form of bits, since computers and computer systems use the binary system. Calculations are made with these numbers to modify them and convert them into an incomprehensible code.

The product of this conversion made to a message is known and called cipher text, in comparison with the original message, known as plain text. An important aspect of the process is to ensure that this change from plain text to cipher text can be perfectly processed by the receiver when it is received and decrypted.

THE ACTION of making a message secret or encoding it to hide its content is called encryption. The reverse procedure, which will allow the receiver to recover the original structure of the message, is decryption. In order for both processes to be fully accomplished and fulfilled, what we know as Symmetric Keys for the secret mode and Asymmetric Keys for the public mode are required.

- **Symmetric keys:** Use of certain algorithms to decrypt and encrypt (hide) documents. They are sets of different algorithms that are related to each other to maintain the guarantee of the confidential connection of the information.
- **Asymmetric keys:** They correspond to a mathematical formula that uses two types of keys, one public and the other private. The public key is susceptible to access by anyone, while the private key is one that can only be used by the person who receives the message and is able to decrypt it.

WE CAN SAY that traditionally cryptography is used to hide messages by certain users. Nowadays, and via computers, this function is even more useful, since communications over the Internet circulate through an infrastructure whose reliability and confidentiality cannot be guaranteed. Cryptography is used not only and precisely to protect the privacy of the data, but also to guarantee its integrity and legitimacy.

WHEN AN OUTSIDER (ATTACKER) tries to penetrate the message without knowing the decryption key, we speak of cryptanalysis or cryptanalysis, the term decryption is also used.

IN GENERAL, cryptography is a technique that facilitates the protection of data and documents, working through the handling of ciphers and codes to make them confidential, thus guaranteeing a more secure and reliable circulation through local networks or the Internet. The presence of cryptography in humanity is as old as writing itself. At the time of the Roman Empire, secret codes were used to hide war projects from those who were not supposed to know them. Only those authorized, trusted people who knew such codes were able to decipher the hidden message.

WITH THE ADVENT of the computer and its evolution, cryptography has managed to travel through a wider terrain and easy disclosure of its contents: immediacy and bilaterality, to mention two simple examples. Thanks to technology, cryptography has been modified, used and structured under mathematical algorithms, maintaining the security of its users. Cryptography preserves its integrity on the web, authenticity of the user, sender and receiver, along with the content of the message and its proper access.

. . .

AN ENCRYPTED MESSAGE, using cryptography as a method, must be strictly private, only the sender and the receiver must have the keys that allow them to access and interpret the entire hidden message. A message needs to be subscribed, i.e. the receiver, the person who will receive the message, will be able to verify and verify if the sender is really the person he claims to be and also have the resources to identify if a message could have been intercepted and modified.

THE METHODS HANDLED today by cryptography are quite secure and efficient, they are based on one or more keys. The key is a sequence of characters containing letters, symbols and digits to be converted into a number, used by cryptographic methods to encode and decode messages, as appropriate.

A universal resource or element widely used through the cryptographic process is money, thus giving rise to what we have already seen and know as digital money. Electronic money or digital money, also known as e-money, electronic cash, electronic currency, digital cash or digital currency, refers to money that is issued electronically, through the use of computerized networks, internet and digitally stored value systems such as Bitcoin.

SOME COUNTRIES USE digital money as an authorized payment instrument, establishing the use of a certain currency. Examples of digital money are banking transactions such as deposits, drafts and transfers. This does not have any representative physical unit and its transactions are carried out through the exchange of bits without the traditional need to use metal coins, banknotes or any payment format; without the intervention or participation of any banking or financial entity, it is feasible to execute any transaction of economic funds on the cryptographic platform.

.   .   .

INSTANT and immediate money from any geographic point, direct to the receiver's hands (account). Safe and reliable at just one click, without the need for physical verification or manual verification; that is digital money in our times, money that comes and goes in a hidden and encrypted trip through the web.

Digital money still represents and constitutes an interesting situation in the world of cryptography, the use and management of electronic money is still being carried out on a relatively low scale in comparison with the number of registered users vs. those who are active, since a certain level of uncertainty persists in a significant number of potential prospects.

AT THE GLOBAL and community level, we should highlight the success of the Octopus card system in Hong Kong, which took its first steps as a payment tool for mass transit, making extensive use of a digital money scheme. In addition, Singapore, like Hong Kong, implemented a payment system for public transportation in trains and buses, among others, based on the same type of card.

GRADUALLY, many countries have been incorporating and adding to the use of digital money, under regulations of their governments and central banks, such is the case of the Netherlands: when it stood out with Chipknip, now extinct, Nicaragua with its TUC card and Venezuela with the creation of El Petro.

THERE IS another great payment system very well known and effective that operates in Aisa, specifically in China; it is WeChat that accumulates about one billion users, who through a QR code, make digital money transfers directly and without mediators.

.   .   .

ALL THESE CHANGES, advances and transformations in non-traditional economic processes, have seen an excellent and magnificent opportunity in the overwhelming technological advances that every day we have the opportunity to witness, these; changes, open an extraordinary range of opportunities and a wide door to the increasingly widespread use of various digital currencies already known and many that will continue to appear in the not too distant future. Now, have you ever wondered what is the potential of these currencies and how far they will be able to go?

IN THIS WONDERFUL journey we are taking through money, its history, transformations and modalities, we will take a leap into the future to stop and think a little about its possible implications. We will embark on a futuristic mission in which we will carry more questions than concrete statements. Let us set out on our journey with a positive attitude and without discouragement, inspired by those words once expressed by the renowned French writer Victor Hugo (1802-1885): "The future has many names. For the weak, it is the unattainable. For the fearful, it is the unknown. For the brave, it is opportunity".

IN OUR STARTING point we are made aware that we cannot leave aside the fact that, for some time now, digital currencies exist and are being very well managed, using appropriate channels with great confidence and immediacy. We must take into account that the reserves of commercial banks in central banks and the payments we make with cards and through mobile applications are clear examples of the existence of digital money.

FOR SUCH REASON, it is convenient for us then, to highlight the great progress and technological advances related to Blockchain mechanisms and the effective skill of its outstanding electronic payment systems, making it possible for digital money to enjoy much more prominence in the economy of the future, as cases we see in the present and verifications we have from the past.

A brief tour makes us recreate an important reflection, and that is that our society needs to achieve immediately, perfect the technology at the highest possible level in order to firmly promote the most practical means to help implement the creation of a digital currency for global use. For the present moment we still count on the existing ones, where the Bitcoin represents a valuable example of actuality and outstanding cryptographic function within the computer world. This is how we start to talk about hashing.

THE HASH IS the name given to a particular cryptographic function. These functions have a primary objective: to encode data in order to create a unique string of characters. In this process, the amount of data that is initially entered into the function is not a limiting factor.

Cryptographic hash functions are useful and feasible for ensuring data authenticity, secure password storage and electronic document signatures.

HASH FUNCTIONS ARE of predilected and wide use within Blockchain technology, with the firm purpose of giving and reinforcing security to them. A prime and clear example is Bitcoin, which uses hashes to enable the effective use of cryptocurrency technology.

A hash is a cryptographic operation and function that generates unique and unrepeatable indicators from data and information received. It is like a fingerprint, that unparalleled fingerprint design that every individual carries on their fingers. Hashes form a key part of Blockchain technology and their usefulness is definitely extensive.

THE FIRST RECORDED hash function occurred in 1961, when Wesley Peterson created the Cyclic Redundancy Check function. This first hash function was created to effectively check the correctness of data transmitted over digital networks from an Internet platform and digital storage systems.

THIS FUNCTION WAS, according to Peterson and experts in the field, easy to implement and fast, gained immediate acceptance and is now an industry standard. Thanks to the evolution and growth of informatics and computers, these systems have achieved excellent specialization and increasingly distinction as a cryptographic function.

HASH FUNCTIONS work through a series of complex logical and mathematical processes. These processes are fed into computer software in order to be used from the computer itself. From there, any series of data can be taken, entered into the function and processed.

THE RESULT WILL BE A FIXED-LENGTH string of characters unique to the characters received. It is practically impossible to reverse the process, i.e. from an already formed hash it is methodically impossible to obtain the original data. Thanks to the process of creating hashes, this is a unidirectional procedure, it travels in one direction only.

Let us illustrate the above explanation with a simple example from everyday life, the making of a doughnut.

EACH AND EVERY ingredient would correspond to the data input to the computer. The process of preparing and cooking the doughnut would correspond to the data encoding by the function. At the end we will have a doughnut with a series of unique and unrepeatable characteristics given by its original ingredients. The reverse process, i.e. to arrive at the basic ingredients starting from a doughnut properly elaborated, is impossible.

. . .

PETERSON'S FUNCTION inspired and allowed the creation of new and, of course, better hashes, among which we mention:

- **MD2:** Created in 1989, it is one of the first cryptographic functions in the world. Its creator was Ronald Rivest. This function enjoyed high prestige, security and efficiency at the time, guaranteeing an extreme level of security on the Internet. Its subsequent evolution led to the creation of the MD5 hash function, used in environments where security is not a major concern.
- **RIPEMD:** Created in 1992, it is a cryptographic function for the European RIPE project. Its main function was to replace the then standard function, MD4. Nowadays, it is considered very secure; especially its versions RIPEMD-160, RIPEMD-256 and RIPEMD-320.

- **SHA:** Created in 1993 by the NSA, it is the current standard in cryptographic hashes. NSA created it as an iconic part of its internal project to authenticate electronic documents. The most secure hash functions to date are SHA and its derivatives. SHA-256 stands out for being key in the technology that made possible and gave way to Bitcoin.

CURRENT HASH FUNCTIONS have a sufficiently high level of security, although this does not mean that they are 100% infallible. An important example is the MD5 hash function. Initially, its specifications guaranteed high security and total reliability. Its use became widespread on the Internet to satisfy the need for a useful hashing system to maintain web security. In 1996, this security was breached and the function could be broken, making it obsolete; it was immediately recommended that its use be abandoned.

.   .   .

IN ANOTHER SCENARIO, functions such as RIPEMD-160 and SHA256 are so complex that the security of their functions is nowadays a total guarantee. For example, to break the security of the SHA-256 function, it is estimated that thousands of years would be required, using high-end supercomputers with the most extensive software and hardware update standards.

THE SAME WOULD BE true for the RIPEMD-160 hash function and its subsequent evolutions. All this can be interpreted to mean that both functions continue to provide a high and reliable level of security, being used without fear and without any inconvenience. And although these hash functions are highly secure, the process of researching and developing more complex ones does not stop, its analysts continue to search for ever more powerful and reliable functions.

THANKS TO THEIR GREAT SPEED, efficiency, computational economy and uniqueness, hash functions are widely used within Blockchain technology. So when Satoshi Nakamoto made public his white paper on Bitcoin, he implied and explained why and how he made use of SHA-256 and RIPEMD-160 in Bitcoin. Since then, Blockchain technology has evolved greatly, considering that the technological foundations remain the same. Making use of strong cryptography and hashes to make the technology even more secure, private and even anonymous is practically a mandate for the Blockchain.

THE BIRTH OF BITCOIN .

.   .   .

IT IS QUITE likely that by now a large number of people in the world have heard about Bitcoin and perhaps know something about it. The fact is that the exponential growth of this currency and its manufacture by millions in a matter of a few years is such that it is undoubtedly giving a lot to talk about. It even generates curiosity to want to know how and why the word Bitcoin has even been mentioned in well-known and highly rated TV programs and series.

TO KNOW if it is a trend, a phenomenon, a process of change or just another digital currency, is our task. Knowing its origin, who was its creator and other data that will give us light so that we can handle the term Bitcoin with confidence and perhaps even participate in the global economic process that has generated discussions, topics and forums of global interest, specifically for the movement and news regarding cryptocurrencies.

Bitcoin is simply a cryptocurrency, a virtual currency, supported by its own network. A virtual currency that is governed from the internet, it is abstract and without physical form as all currencies as we know them.

CURRENTLY THERE ARE countless businesses around the world that accept public, open and direct payment of their operations through Bitcoin.

IN 2008 BITCOIN was created by a person who became known under the pseudonym Satoshi Nakamoto, whose specific identification is still unknown. Together with a group of volunteer developers, Nakamoto worked on a source code of applications until December 2010, when he ceased his public activity.

. . .

BERNARD VON NOTHAUS was an inspiration for Satoshi Nakamoto, remember that years ago Nakamoto contacted him to let him know his great admiration for the feat of having created his own currency and that he would take the same step, creating the Bitcoin soon after.

BITCOIN IS a self-regulated payment unit with no backing, no physical reference and no endorsement by any country that keeps the identity of its owners anonymous. Its operations and other transactions are carried out through the Internet by means of encrypted codes and confirmed in multiple ways by the participants and members of the technological network known as Blockchain.

The knowledge and possession of a code makes whoever acquires it, the owner of such asset (cryptocurrency). Bitcoin is a purely digital currency. Among the most controversial aspects surrounding Bitcoin is its creation process, which is known and described as mining. In practice, this process has come to be controlled by very few hands, most of which are duly organized groups established in Asia. With the constant growth in the price of Bitcoin, the profitability of its mining process is only possible in geographic regions where energy costs are lower.

THIS CURRENCY IS a concrete version of cash that uses cryptography to have total control over its creation and operations, far from a centralized power, and unlike fiat money, its value is not established by any monetary authority that issues it.

FOR MANY, Bitcoin is a complete mystery as the identity of its creator, for others the opportunity to replace the current financial system. For governments it is a means through which organized crime can carry out its operations without being detected, but for investors, Bitcoin is the new virtual currency that cannot be missing in any business and investment portfolio.

Bitcoin (BTC) is the first digital currency used and distributed in virtual form, whose value in the first days of April 2021 reached 58,806.23 US dollars, is itself a decentralized peer-to-peer network. There is no institution or person worldwide that controls its issuance, expenditure or reserve. The production of each Bitcoin is digital and only 21 million units exist. Its creator is said to own 5% of them.

THE PROGRAMMER SATOSHI NAKAMOTO and his group of programmers, presented for the first time in 2009, an open source software called Bitcoin, product of the economic crisis that the financial sector was going through due to the well-known real estate bubble and the consequent decision taken by governments to print excessive inorganic money to protect and rescue banks.

MANY DOUBTS and rumors persist about the true identity of Satoshi Nakamoto, creator of Bitcoin, however, each and every person associated with these rumors has denied being Nakamoto. On one occasion, in 2012, Nakamoto himself claimed to be a 37 year old male, residing in Japan, which was not entirely convincing because he spoke perfect and very fluent English, and also raised concerns about the schedule he set to connect to network forums and the software he used was not labeled in Japanese.

HOW WERE CRYPTOCURRENCIES CREATED?

FROM ITS ORIGIN two notions can be distinguished within the same term Cryptocurrency. Crypto is the first one, and it is based on cryptography, which according to the RAE means to write with a secret key or in an enigmatic way; and Currency, the second one.

. . .

IN THIS SENSE, when Wei Dai first spread the concept of crypto-graphic currency on the "cypherpunks" mailing list in 1998, he proposed the conjunction or pairing of a new currency and cryptog-raphy with the aim of replacing the control performed by a central-ized monetary authority in the generation or creation and execution of its operations through the encrypted use of mathematical proofs and tests that provide high and guaranteed levels of security.

LIKE MOST INVENTIONS AND INNOVATIONS, the first cryptocurrency to appear required a gestation and maturation time and an appropriate context. Therefore, one month after the Lehman Brothers bank-ruptcy, Satoshi Nakamoto published on October 31, 2008 the first whitepaper on his first cryptocurrency called "Bitcoin (₿, BTC, XBT), A Peer-to-Peer (P2P) Electronic Cash System"- "Bitcoin (₿, BTC, XBT), A Peer-to-Peer (P2P) Electronic Cash System"- "A Peer-to-Peer (P2P) Electronic Cash System".

THE WHITEPAPER PROPOSES the creation of an electronic payment operating system without the need for an intermediary or supervi-sory authority to provide confidence in the ownership of each user's monetary units. To this end, it recognizes the importance and neces-sity of implementing a chronological record of all operations and transactions in order to elucidate their existence, and the subsequent transmission to all other servers in the network in order to avoid any risk of double spending of the units.

IN THIS WAY, because the transaction records are associated or grouped in blocks that contain all the data and information of the previous block, a blockchain, called Blockchain, is created.

. . .

BY THE END of January 2009, Satoshi Nakamoto announces to the world and makes official through the network, the launch of his creation: Bitcoin, the first cryptographic currency in history and that would become the genesis of a new and unprecedented way of trading on the network through the web.

IT IS VERY INTERESTING, talking about the origin of virtual currencies, to highlight that, to date, and 12 years after Bitcoin, the most notable, relevant and important cryptocurrency in the world, was created and made known to the world; there are approximately more than 1600 digital currencies on the network that seek to cover and satisfy the countless needs of millions of users who today use this innovative resource as their first line financial resource.

CHARACTERISTICS OF THE BITCOIN NETWORK.

WE HAVE SEEN the historical moment and the circumstances that were present in the world when Bitcoin was created and made known as an open source software and its appearance as the first digital currency, as well as a number of important aspects regarding its structure, operation, effectiveness, security and value. Let's learn a little more about this fascinating currency and some of its basic characteristics.

- **It is anonymous:** Banks have sufficient knowledge about all their customers' data. Addresses, phone numbers, emails, contact references, workplaces, balances, other accounts, expenses, movements and much more. The same is true of Google and Facebook, networks that can track all user information with just a couple of clicks. With the use of the Bitcoin network, everything is different,

since the wallets used by its millions of users to make
expenses and purchases, are not linked to any personal
information thanks to its cryptographic quality.

- **Transparent:** Each and every transaction made within the
Bitcoin Blockchain network is safeguarded in a Public
Ledger that is recorded in the Blockchain itself and is
openly visible. This means that all activities within the
network are perceptible, with no possibility of being able
to trace the individual ownership of each Bitcoin held by
people within the network.

- **Fast:** All transactions carried out within the Bitcoin
Blockchain network can be resolved in just minutes, with
no limitations on the location of the parties involved in the
transaction in question. If we compare an urgent situation
suffered by national or international banking services with
Bitcoin; we will see the extreme speed with which Bitcoin
has, a considerable advantage since speed in the execution
of their actions.

- **Irreversible:** Carrying out a transaction with no way back.
Once users participate in the closing of a transaction
within the Bitcoin Blockchain network, there is no way for
it to be reversed. This is a feature that can be considered a
double-edged sword, and should be used with caution,
precision and care. Its positive side lies in the fact that we
can be completely sure that each Bitcoin we receive
cannot be returned to the person who sent it to us, but we
must be prudent and cautious when we send Bitcoins to
the precise address, we must verify that it is the correct
one. It is advisable to verify that all the data is in order
before making any type of operation.

ONLY FOUR CHARACTERISTICS that deserve special observation and
attention, as well as the scientific method and all circumstances of
daily life: Observation. Look carefully and proceed with prudence.

· · ·

THE UNIQUE BACKING that this currency has is represented by the technological algorithms, which since its creation have been impossible to penetrate, although the risk exists. A great quality of Bitcoin is that it is a cryptocurrency that under no condition can be intercepted or the possibility of seeing frozen accounts in this currency, in addition to the fact that it is required to give identity data when making negotiations with Bitcoins. It is quite likely to have a high volatility of its price, due to its speculative crater and its fluctuating movement of supply and demand.

THE BITCOIN BLOCKCHAIN NETWORK, as we have seen, is a very secure and reliable network that enjoys private and guaranteed operation, providing discretion to its users, in addition to generating a unique and important economic growth within the capital market. Given its status as a decentralized digital currency that cannot be counterfeited, thanks to the excellent defense mechanisms integrated within each algorithm used in the same network, it increases its level of trust.

BITCOIN IS a currency of eternal durability. Yes, as you read it. Because a Bitcoin does not exist in physical form, it means that it can never be damaged, broken or altered. A Bitcoin can be kept permanently on the internet without any problems.

THE MYSTERIOUS CREATOR OF BITCOIN.
Who was really Satoshi Nakamoto?

SATOSHI NAKAMOTO WAS BORN in Japan on April 5, 1975. He is a mathematician and cryptographer creator of the open source network Bitcoin and the first digital currency Bitcoin. He has a net worth of 1,000,000.00BTC of Bitcoins (58,823,000,000,000.00$ US dollars calculated as of April 2021), recognized in 2015 with the Innovation Award by The Economist and proposed nomination for the Nobel Prize in Economics in 2016 but rejected by the Royal Swedish Academy of Sciences, since, if the laureate is deceased or anonymous, it is not awarded.

BY 2012, in his P2P (Peer-To-Peer) Foundation profile, Satoshi Nakamoto claimed to be a 37-year-old man, residing in Japan, without specifying any additional information about city or other geographic data. Many doubted his words because of his impeccable English and the fact that his Bitcoin software was not labeled or documented in Japanese.

In a thorough work developed by researcher Dan Kaminsky, who analyzed in depth the Bitcoin open source network, it was expressed that Satoshi Nakamoto might not be the person he claimed to be and who would present himself in his P2P profile. Nakamoto could be a group or work team made up of very well-organized programmers. All this merited Kaminsky to consider Nakamoto as a genius.

A developer who was part of the Bitcoin team from its beginnings stated that he was in constant contact with Nakamoto via e-mail and considered that his communication code was too well developed to believe that he was communicating with a single person.

FOR MANY RESEARCHERS, given the task of trying to find the possibility of contacting the identity of Satoshi Nakamoto, the idea that Nakamoto is a native of a country belonging to the Commonwealth is supported by the eventual use of British English terms and grammar found in his source code and in the messages of his forums.

A SERIES of investigative data and interesting analyses provided by Swiss programmer and community member Stefan Thomas concluded that the times of each of the more than 500 messages posted by Nakamoto on the Bitcoin forum showed a significant drop between 5:00 am and 11:00 am Greenwich Mean Time on the resulting graph.

THIS SEQUENCE REMAINED UNCHANGED, even on weekends; this allowed Thomas to calculate that the genius creator of Bitcoin would be in normal sleeping hours, asleep at those times. Considering the above and if Nakamoto is a single person, with conventional sleeping habits, then he could be found in some region in the UTC-5 or UTC-6 time zone; North American populations in North American Eastern Standard Time and Central Standard Time, in Central American, Caribbean and South American locations.

APART FROM ALL THIS set of hypotheses, because so far they are just that; hypotheses, there are countless investigations circulating around the brilliant mind of the Bitcoin, its identity and its location somewhere in the world. Again, it is believed that Satoshi Nakamoto may be a person or a group or community of individuals who make a professional life for the Bitcoin network.

THERE ARE real names of people who are part of the network and some of them are presumed to be the real Nakamoto:

- Nick Szabo
- Dorian Nakamoto
- Hal Finney
- Craig Steven Wright
- Vincent van Volkmer

CRYPTOCURRENCY EXPERTS and researchers agree on the same argument, and that is that the work of the Bitcoin open source network is so well done, developed, executed and assembled, that it would be somewhat difficult to attribute all the credit to the effort and fruit of a single person.

A LARGE GALLERY of names has been paraded around pointing to possible candidates to be the real Nakamoto, many have been dismissed as unlikely to be. By 2011 Joshua Davis had set his sights on Finnish sociologist and economist Vili Lehdonvirta and Irish student Michael Claro, which he reported in an article, published in The New Yorker; however, both denied such attributions.

THAT SAME YEAR, Adam Penenberg, an investigative journalist, referred to Neal Rey, Vladimir Oksman and Charles Bry as the possible creators of Bitcoin, since in 2008 these people filed a patent that in one of its texts contained the phrase: "computationally impracticable to reverse", the same expression that would also appear in the Bitcoin White Paper, and three days later the domain bitcoin.org was registered. However, all this was no mere coincidence, as these three people denied any connection with the emerging cryptocurrency.

TWO YEARS LATER, in May 2013, Ted Nelson, the Internet pioneer, suggested in a video that Shinichi Mochizuki could be Nakamoto, denying such a claim a few days later. For that same year, Israeli mathematicians Adi Shamir and Dorit Ron, found a certain link between Satoshi Nakamoto and Ross Ulbritch, recognized creator of the Darknet Silk Road market, being one of the first to accept cryptocurrencies as a means of payment, who later retracted such claims.

IN 2015, Travis Patron, a prominent researcher, insinuated the Nobel Prize winner in economics John Forbes Nash, given his high knowledge in the concept of money, besides being a brilliant mind who shared several points of view in common with Bitcoin. More recently, on November 2017, a rumor began to circulate making believe that the renowned inventor and entrepreneur Elon Musk, could be the true creator of Bitcoin, but he immediately proceeded to deny such idea.

THE SAME THING happened at the beginning of 2018, Nigerian developer Mark Essien published a theory of his own claiming that Bram Cohen, the creator of BitTorrent if it would be Satoshi Nakamoto, based on circumstantial evidence.

One thing we can say with total certainty is that, under the alias of Satoshi Nakamoto, a person or a group of programmers, is the creator of Bitcoin, a real transformation in the use of money since 2009 with its new and first digital currency.

WITH ALL THE investigations carried out for more than 20 years to find the identity of this emblematic character and all the failed results, we can assure the growth of a digital currency that still keeps secret for the whole world society the name of its progenitor; while with a little more than 100 million users trust more and more in this solid currency and its preponderant growth as an outstanding resource of value.

AS LONG AS the trust towards Bitcoin continues to grow, based on its advanced platform, from its own Blockchain network, this currency will remain latent in the global cryptographic market, giving greater guarantee to the operations with real electronic money. We can assure and reiterate that the trust and solidity of the projects is the basis for the success of this impressive cryptocurrency.

· · ·

WHAT ARE BITCOINS?

WE HAVE SEEN CONCEPTS, definitions, characteristics, extensive details and various explanatory aspects about Bitcoins, which will never be enough, especially when it comes to this influential element representative of the new economies.

BITCOINS IS a virtual currency or also an electronic resource of exchange, valid and useful to acquire products, goods and services as we do with any other currency. In addition, it is a decentralized currency, there is no authority, bank or government that assumes responsibility, control or authority over it, manages its issuance or represents any power in their records and movements. It should be noted that Bitcoin consists of a cryptographic key intimately associated with a virtual wallet, which debits and receives payments.

THIS IS A PURELY virtual type of money, as if it were traditional banknotes and coins in an online version, since with it you can buy and pay for the same things; from a cup of coffee to a mansion. Its popularity has grown so much that there are already many establishments, stores, companies and businesses that accept it as a means of payment.

AN ILLUSTRATIVE IMAGE of Bitcoin or how this currency looks in physical form, can only be seen in graphic designs for photos or videos, since the currency as such does not exist in palpable exchange format, they are only formats that help to have an idea of how it would look or would be the Bitcoin. There are many high value items in the world such as gold, silver and diamonds.

.   .   .

YOU MAY WONDER why Bitcoin is worth so much. This is worth more every day because people are and remain willing to pay and exchange it even for goods and services, even for real money. As long as this currency continues to be decentralized and free of external ties, more users will be willing to join and join its network.

BITCOIN IS a strong currency that has experienced astonishing rises, however, it has also suffered significant drops since more than a decade ago when it was created. Knowledgeable critics consider that changing all your real money to Bitcoins is not entirely safe, because the risk you would incur could perhaps be too high. However, this cryptocurrency continues to gain more and more followers, it is gaining favor with a wide audience, despite years of skepticism for many.

DAY AFTER DAY Bitcoin is getting stronger and gaining followers as important and well-known as Uber or Mastercard, the rapper Jay Z or the president of Twitter Jack Dorsey, and even Tesla, who announced having invested 1,500 million dollars in the purchase of Bitcoin and will soon begin to accept the cryptocurrency as a form of payment in the sale of their vehicles.

Bitcoin is a currency of inestimable growth and financial impact.

We have then that Bitcoin is a digital currency or decentralized cryptocurrency that can be used to exchange goods and services in places where it is accepted, just as we do with any other legal tender fiat currency. Bitcoin's symbol is ₿ and its abbreviation BTC or XBT. It is a free electronic currency that allows direct transactions without any type of intermediary or mediators.

LET'S remember that Bitcoin (₿, BTC, XBT) was created in 2009, together with the software that supports it, by the person who calls himself Satoshi Nakamoto, currently a possible individual or group of people?

To this day this remains a mystery, since it is unknown who is really behind that name, whether a person or institution. Bitcoins are created through a process known as Bitcoin mining.

WHAT IS the purpose of Bitcoin?

BEFORE GOING into the basics of what the purpose of Bitcoin is, let's refresh a little bit on how money works, so it will be much easier to understand why this cryptocurrency exists.

When you accept to perform a certain job, you will be admitting some condition proposed by the other person, who has offered you a certain amount of money in exchange for it. Here the money will be representing the work we have agreed to do to this person.

This money will be used in the purchase of products that you wish to acquire, with which you will be paying in a store with the money that you received for your work, in this way that money will continue successively in movement and changing hands frequently. It is traditional money issued by the government that you will handle physically or through cards and also transfers, it is the official legal tender.

UNDERSTANDING THE POINT, let's see a delicate and strong aspect that these currencies have to live; their weakness against counterfeiting, despite the great efforts and design tasks that governments devote to produce money with a paper currency difficult to replicate or perhaps impossible to duplicate, in addition to relying on banking and payment platforms available digitally, before all this; our economic and financial system depends entirely on third parties.

. . .

WELL, none of this happens with the figure of cryptocurrencies, whose philosophy is completely different and has no dependence on any authority for its creation, administration and management. The cost of the traditional banking system is too high, especially when international operations are carried out, there are governments that do not stop printing money, such is the case of Venezuela; which simply produces higher inflation and alteration of data, depending on these entities is costly for society. A cryptocurrency such as Bitcoin aims to eliminate these expenses. But it is not just about expenses, purchases and sales.

IN THE YEARS of Bitcoin's existence, we have witnessed its expansion and growth in value as a cryptocurrency, however, it has not been easy to capture the attention of the general community necessary to understand the usefulness of its technology and the objectives pursued.

EDUCATE: the user and the community in general: This is the main task Bitcoin has as a cryptocurrency appearing available on the network. Promote a broad education about its benefits, advantages and weaknesses. Keep the prospect interested in being part of the network on how it works and what opportunities the cryptocurrency offers in the economic sphere within a very well protected digital system.

ORIENTATION: to those who want to join the community: Providing information about the possibilities offered by Bitcoin as a decentralized digital currency, providing guidance for those who already have experience in the field or for those who want to start, receiving some specific information.

. . .

OFFERING TECHNOLOGICAL ADVANCEMENT: Bitcoin has a secure and reliable platform. Its high technological support makes it practically impenetrable, which is a guarantee of trust in its community.

- Business adoption: Seek to achieve greater economic importance as it becomes part of the commercial and business framework. Even as its value increases, Bitcoin seeks strategies that will allow it to occupy a space in the commercial sphere. Among Bitcoin's objectives, it is closely related to the well-known "altcoins", the alternative currencies in charge of offering solutions to the commercial problems derived from this fourth industrial revolution. At this point Bitcoin seeks to take its place at the core of this new market, in which much of the activity is digital and automated.

INCREASING INTEROPERABILITY: One of its priority objectives, which should receive special attention in the future, is to expand its presence in networks, since there is still very little communication between them and this could even result in the unjustified loss of money due to easily correctable errors. Every network is independent of another and has its own characteristics and particularities. However, the emergence of new upgrades can facilitate operations and connectivity between networks much more. In this way it will be possible and guaranteed the creation of a favorable commercial environment that will allow to obtain greater versatility for the monetary use of the very varied cryptoassets.

CREATION OF SERVICES: To found in the immediate future a whole environment of services around the technology. Storage services, insurance services, simple mobile applications, support centers to provide technological support to new businesses in their adaptation, among others. Creations that would make and consider Bitcoin as a reference asset in the current economic system.

. . .

COMPANIES and financial institutions would begin to encourage the use of crypto-related products and services, given the tendency to see cryptocurrencies as a means to trade or make more money. Undoubtedly, Bitcoin and other digital currencies are an excellent resource to generate income, but they are bound to be given more value for their ability to offer business solutions than for their possibilities as a speculative commodity.

EASY AND FRIENDLY USE: Day by day it is easier and easier to enter Bitcoin and invest in it, as with any other cryptocurrency, however, there is a long and profitable way to go in terms of usability. There are numerous intuitive platforms in the market in which, interested people can acquire, exchange and trade with Bitcoin; however, certain technical knowledge is still necessary to allow and guarantee a correct use of the tool and this type of digital currencies. This and more can be achieved by facilitating a massive adoption of the technology, through the emergence of new applications and companies that make it truly easy to accept cryptocurrencies in their own business with the possibility of storing and securing them.

THE BASIC OBJECTIVES of Bitcoin are to make cryptocurrencies and their Blockchain technology a good for the benefit of all mankind. Much of society is not yet prepared and ready to face the next industrial revolution from an ideological and intellectual point of view. As with all past industrial revolutions, there will be its detractors and a large number of people closed to change and new technological and professional trends. In this respect, guidance, education and support from organizations is essential and fundamental. The great advances in technology always manage to impose themselves thanks to their demonstrated and proven usefulness by a small group of users to whom merit is also due for recognizing and allowing themselves to take a step forward, in the face of the changes that arise in society.

· · ·

How does Bitcoin work?

Bitcoin is a cryptocurrency that works through digital wallets, which use a private key that allows access and execution of all its applications. Payments and other transactions are made from its platform through the internet and through a cryptographic protection system, protected by the Blockchain network.

In order to operate and manage Bitcoin effectively, it is enough to download any of the available applications offered in any desktop or mobile operating system. This can be iOS or Android (MultiBit or Bitcoin Wallet).

Once you have downloaded the application, you will be able to create your Bitcoin wallet which, in a nutshell; consists of a private key in conjunction with a public key, which will allow you to perform your operations. Thanks to these keys, Bitcoins cannot be counterfeited, thus guaranteeing the legitimacy, security and protection of all transactions made between users.

The Bitcoin cryptocurrency system uses a cryptographic public key for access. A coin has the owner's public key. When a coin is transferred from user A to user B, A attaches B's public key to the coin, which will then be signed with A's private key. User B then has the coin credited to him, which he can transfer at any time he wishes.

Once user A carries out the operation, he will not be able to receive again the same currency he has just transferred, since the network keeps a record of all the operations that are carried out collectively through a public list.

With the immense number of registered users, close to 1 billion people, Bitcoin has become the most widely used cryptocurrency in the world today. Bitcoin allows you to reduce amounts that usually represent large amounts when making substantial transactions.

By LOGGING in you can view your balance or account statement, with the possibility of using it, transferring Bitcoin to another account only with the requested data. Bitcoin performs all its activity in a fast, safe and secure way, directly and immediately between the digital wallets of the users participating in the negotiation, verified through the Blockchain network; considering the veracity of the digital signatures with corresponding keys demonstrating the authenticity of the owners of the wallets.

THROUGH BLOCKCHAIN, Bitcoin performs a decentralized public registry. That is, a certain number of transactions form a database unit known as "Blocks". Each of these blocks has the possibility of storing information from the previous block, just as each transaction collects information about its preceding transaction. In this way, the blockchain provides full transparency of all your payments and movements.

THE BITCOIN ECOSYSTEM.
   Blockchain is the ecosystem for Bitcoin.

A WORD that we have mentioned about twenty times and that we have not explained in detail. When we talk about ecosystem, it immediately comes to mind a biological system made up of living organisms that inhabit and coexist in the same physical space. Something similar is the coexistence environment for a digital structure that requires its place of seating and coexistence, its home or center of operations.

. . .

WHEN WE SPEAK of a blockchain ecosystem, we refer to the parts that make up the whole and how those parts interact with each other and in turn with its external world.

THE BITCOIN ECOSYSTEM, the case of our interest; boils down to four important parts:

- Users: Those who receive and send payments.
- Miners: Those who generate the cryptocurrencies.
- Investors: Those who buy them.
- Developers: Those who supervise and support all of the above.

NONE of the parts that make up the equation could work without the others being there as well, all together in this important support community. In any case, a valuable set of components must work properly and adequately; in a single word, it must work well to keep a Blockchain project operational.

BLOCKCHAIN IS the technological basis on which the Bitcoin mining and quoting process is supported, a processing that allows users of this cryptocurrency to make payments and transactions in an encrypted and authenticated manner in a distributed database.

ANY TOPIC RELATED to Bitcoin will be closely related and linked to Blockchain, being this the technology in which the cryptocurrency is supported. In conclusion, it is a large distributed database on multiple servers around the world that gathers all transactions that occur with Bitcoin.

.   .   .

EACH AND EVERY one of these encrypted and authenticated operations are added to the blockchain, better known as Blockchain, on which Bitcoin is based, a process impossible to carry out without APIs, a set of commands, functions and computer protocols that allow developers to create specific programs for certain operating systems.

AN ADDED value and of excellent organic impedance is the interest that Bitcoin technology is awakening among developers on a daily basis, if we compare it with platforms or other online payment systems such as PayPal. At present, there are about 3,200 PayPal-related repositories incorporated in the collaborative development platform GitHub, compared to those linked to Bitcoin, which total more than 8,000 repositories.

THE ENTIRE PROCESS OF OPERATIONS, procedures, reception, issuance of payments with virtual wallets or data management is possible thanks to the existence of a development interface for applications for each of its functions. Blockchain has several APIs for different functionalities. Without them or with the absence of some of them, it would simply be impossible to carry out any kind of activity or operations with Bitcoin in the world.

THE BLOCKCHAIN TECHNOLOGICAL system allows the execution of value transactions between users without the need for intervention of third parties or intermediaries at any stage of the process, i.e., the management of transactions is completely decentralized and gives all its members the same ledger or what is the same, a decentralized database (distributed ledger).

TRANSACTIONS CAN BE in digital currencies (cryptocurrencies) or under any other modality: (goods, information, services, etc.) and are developed on platforms in which its nodes communicate through peer-to-peer networks (Peer-To-Peer) via Internet connections.

THE BLOCKCHAIN OFFERS a dynamic and unalterable representation or record of its operations over time that replaces intermediaries and centralized trust authorities such as managers, banks, notaries, insurers, etc. that support transactions by the digital trust that users have placed in this advanced and high-level technology.

THE BLOCKCHAIN OFFERS all its participants total transparency behind a reliable protocol (all users have access to all the information stored in the distributed database), sharing and decentralization, or what is the same; the same duplicate of the database in all nodes.

THE BLOCKCHAIN IS IRREVERSIBLE, meaning that once a piece of data is recorded, it cannot be altered or deleted.

No intermediation, no central arbiter to supervise the movements. Participants make their decisions with full and free consensus or determination.

The blockchain links the entire series of transactions and incorporates a "timestamp" that gives clarity and traceability to the procedures without transgressing a priori the privacy of users. There is ease of knowledge of the path and content, but it is not always feasible to infer on the identity of the user.

Participants have the opportunity to adopt three roles: users with the open right to consult a copy of the shared database (accessors), participants with the freedom to perform transactions (Participants) and users in charge of validating and confirming operations and creating blocks (Miner).

All with the possibility of a validated and unique copy of the database.

. . .

SOME APIs within the Bitcoin ecosystem:

RECEIVE PAYMENTS API: Version 2 of this interface has been available since January 1, 2016. In a simple way it allows a company or business to start accepting automated payments in Bitcoin. The API is based on HTTP GET requests and its main objective is to create a unique address for each user and for each invoice issue for each Bitcoin transaction. A prerequisite for a good and guaranteed practice.

BLOCKCHAIN WALLET API: As of January 1, 2019, it is necessary to install a local server for the management of the virtual wallet and thus make use of this API. A HTTP, POST or GET call base is the communication method used by it. The process by which a virtual wallet is created is called create_wallet. Each created wallet is linked to a password with a minimum length of 10 characters, an API authenticity code, a private key per user, a folder where the wallet was created and an email address.

JSON RPC API: Enabled since March 2016. The universal suggestion commended to all Bitcoin users is to use the novel Blockchain Wallet API, very despite the fact that the interface calls are RPC-based, it is still akin to the past Bitcoin RPC protocol for generating interaction with virtual wallets.

THE API CAN BE INSTALLED and used from libraries in a wide range of programming languages: syntaxes such as Python, Ruby, PHP, Node.js and .NET.

Other APIs:

- Blockchain Data API

- Query API
- WebSocket API
- Exchange Rates API
- Chars & Statistics API

WHOEVER WISHES to use Bitcoin is free and ready to do so, the basic and necessary thing is to install a virtual wallet on a device. It is not necessary to have excessive knowledge and full mastery of technical and technological aspects to get started in the use of this precious cryptocurrency, since it works just like any other digital currency and online payment processing.

IT SHOULD BE NOTED that each transaction made by the user through Bitcoin, after verified, is added to the blockchain, from then on the user will become part of an accounting record shared by other users.

A CONSTITUTION of elements and resources in full and constant interaction, make up the fascinating Bitcoin ecosystem from Blockchain, guaranteeing exceptional, secure, timely and universal functionality, reaching any user globally with total guarantee and protection.

BITCOIN MINING

BITCOIN IS a network of computers all connected to each other. It is a flat topology network, which means that all the interlinked computers act with the same level of importance, although it is likely that there may be some differences between them.

ALL THESE COMPUTERS connected in a network and in the same hierarchical scheme, perform at the same time the same type of operations, something as simple as propagating among them the transactions that the node itself (in the Bitcoin context usually refers to a computer that has downloaded the Bitcoin-QT or Bitcoin Core software to participate in the peer-to-peer network), or other nodes generate and any other communication.

ALL THESE COMPUTERS are simultaneously and at the same time client and server, making requests or requests, in the same way when we visit a web page, giving instantaneously and together, response to requests received. Something like when you look to visit bitcoin.org and its server sends you its page. This means that Bitcoin computers communicate with each other 24/7 and "talk" constantly following the rules of the Bitcoin protocol.

BITCOIN MINING IS DESIGNED with the firm intention of being itself a resource intensive and difficulty intensive resource, so that the number of blocks received by the miners remains intact and unchanged. Each and every one of these individual blocks must contain a Proof of Work in order to be qualified and considered valid. This Proof of Work is verified and confirmed by other Bitcoin nodes each time a new block is received. Bitcoin relies on the use of Hash-Cash as its primary Proof of Work function.

THE MAIN PURPOSE of Bitcoin mining is to allow its nodes to achieve a way to reach a secure and tamper-resistant consensus. Mining is also the very mechanism used to introduce Bitcoins into the system. Miners are paid for their transaction fees as something like a "subsidy" of newly created coins.

THIS PROCESS IS CALLED Bitcoin mining because of its resemblance to the mining of other commodities, which requires effort to slowly obtain a new coin that will be available at a price that resembles the rate at which raw materials are mined, such as gold is mined from the earth.

WITHIN THE BLOCKCHAIN SYSTEM, the ones in charge of generating new blocks are the miners, who add them at the end of each chain. And as established in the Bitcoin protocols, they must perform this procedure every 10 minutes on average. Each of the mined blocks contains a detailed record of different transactions carried out in each suggested time period. Once added to the end of the Blockchain, they update their record. As can be illustrated, it is a continuous and unstoppable process.

BLOCK MINING PROCESS.

TO PRODUCE or create a new block, the miners in charge of this activity must solve important mathematical difficulties. Upon finding the effective result valid for the network, a new block is considered mined. This reward is known as "The Block Reward".

APPROXIMATELY EVERY 10 minutes a new block is created in Bitcoin. So every time one block is found, mining starts for another block, since they are mathematically connected or concatenated with each other.

TRANSACTION:

THE MINING PROCESS that will give rise to a new block starts the moment a user decides to send an estimated amount in cryptocurrencies to another user. To do so, the user sends the transaction in question with all its data from the wallet, while waiting for the necessary response time for the network to process and approve the transaction. In that block they will remain while it is time for the next one to be mined where they can be included and validated.

COMPILATION:

THE TRANSACTIONS that remain deferred or under pending status in the network, will be selected to then form groups in a block of transactions by the mining nodes. There is, and is given the possibility of different miners holding the same transactions at the same time, but these will be without confirmation or approval until the next block is mined.

FORMATION:

THE TRANSACTIONS INCLUDED to form and then mine a new block, are personally selected by each miner. In the event that there are transactions that have been validated and already included in a new block, they will be eliminated from this other block. The new block is known as a candidate, since it has not been approved because it does not have the validity of a proof of work.

When a new block is formed, it is imperative to include in it a header that must contain the hash of the previous block, the Merkle root and the data and information required for the mining competition. That is, it needs to include the timestamp, the purpose of the PoW algorithm for the block, software version and the nonce.

PROOF OF WORK:

· · ·

FOR EACH BLOCK that has been formed by its respective miner, a valid signature must be searched for, this is called the proof of work. Each particular block formed goes through a mathematical calculation process that is performed by its respective miner. Thus, if the procedure is the same, the result will be completely different and unique for each block. There is a lot of computational power in this complex calculation process, generating an excessive consumption of electrical energy that will depend proportionally on the difficulty of the system for its mining moment.

Each miner searches for its solution, this solution is called a hash. It is a complex function to find, however, once found it is quite easy to verify through the other nodes. In this way it will be possible to verify that the output hash meets all the conditions set by the system.

Finding an output hash results in arduous and repetitive mathematical calculations performed by the miners over and over again through a nonce, a random character number used and changed frequently until a valid signature or output hash is found according to the condition of the case. There is no way to predict which nonce will solve the problem, so as many and as many as necessary must be used. This situation is for billions of securities.

IN THE CASE of the Bitcoin network, its system stipulates that each output hash must contain a certain number of leading zeros in its structure.

TRANSMISSION:

ONCE THE MINING node manages to come up with a valid output hash in favor of a block, this is transmitted attached to the signature with the other nodes in the network so that all manage to be validated.

Currently, and as long as 21 million Bitcoins have not been issued, as mentioned above, each miner receives his reward, which is established by the mining, placing new Bitcoins in circulation. All this is recorded in their own nodes, the other nodes in the network will do it in the next step.

All miners will receive the respective mining commissions that Bitcoin users have placed in their operations that set up the block; regardless of whether or not all Bitcoins have been issued.

VERIFICATION:

THE REMAINING nodes of the network will be in charge of verifying and validating that both the block and the hash, comply with all the conditions of the system, corroborating its legitimacy and verifying if it indeed contains the amount that is established by the network.

VERIFICATION ALSO RATIFIES the Proof of Work, this translates into the computational power consumed to find the solution, giving credit to the miner who discovered the block who will undoubtedly be able to make free use of the Bitcoins just received.

CONFIRMATION:

Once the new block is uploaded to the blockchain, the following blocks that are included over it will be considered as confirmed. In this case, we could have in mind the possibility that each miner, when starting the process with a block of his property, can continue with the mining process. This is not the case. When a new block is generated, the mining nodes are structured to start the process by forming a new transaction block. It is not feasible to continue mining from a previously formed block, because each block must receive the hash that corresponds to the block that precedes it.

This is why the technology is known as blockchain. Thus, when the miner manages to get the required valid hash, another set of new blocks could have been mined for sure. Thus, the output hash of his already mined block will not be able to match the output hash of the last block that was added to the chain, it would be rejected. In addition, it is quite likely that the transactions, or most of them, contained in the block in question have been added to others. Even if the block is successfully mined, most of its transactions will be rejected and invalidated.

BITCOIN IN PRACTICE:

THIS CRYPTOCURRENCY APPEARS as a reliable resource for the payment of products, services and goods without the participation of third parties. The possibility of acquiring Bitcoins can be practical and simple, and its acceptance by commercial establishments, businesses and physical stores is becoming wider and wider.

The first recognized operation or transaction that constituted the first great value for the nascent Bitcoin was the purchase of a couple of pizzas at the Papa John's chain. In that digital negotiation, 10,000BTC were transferred, which represented in fiat money the amount of 30$USD. The vote of confidence placed by this food chain and Laszlo Haynek's interest in using his digital Bitcoin wallet, invited an incalculable number of physical and digital stores to be part of this network experience.

TRAVEL, Tourism, Leisure and Free Time

IF YOU ARE THINKING about traveling, you are planning your next vacation, you want to take a cruise or relive your unforgettable Honeymoon, paying with your Bitcoins, here is a list of tourism specialists, willing to make your dream come true... Using your cryptocurrencies!

. . .

DESTINIA:

Spanish Travel and Tourism company offering packages, accommodations, air services, cruises and getaways; accepts payments in Bitcoin and Bitcoin Cash .

13TICKETS:

Ticket sales for all kinds of events and that reached an agreement with Real Madrid to offer visitors, tickets for a tour of the Santiago Bernabeu, paying via Bitcoins.

VIRGIN GALACTIC:

If your travel illusion in these new vacations is to live an extreme experience and reach heights beyond a normal flight, Virgin Galactic is the answer. Reach the atmosphere and make your payments on the network using Bitcoins.

CHEAPAIR:

A company dedicated to the promotion, booking and sale through the internet of air services, car rental and hotel reservations around the world, makes available to its customers its updated payment platform through Bitcoin.

ATOM TRAVEL:

Tourism wholesaler with over 30 years of experience in the industry, offers design, planning development of tourism services at all levels, with the best regional correspondents in hotels, vehicles, cruises, parks and flights, has its own platform for payments in Bitcoins.

. . .

VIDEO GAMES

FOR FANS of video games and those who wish to have on their computers and digital distraction devices, many companies dedicated to this area make available to their secure customers through the web, a wide variety of games that can be purchased by payment under the Bitcoin platform.

IT SHOULD BE NOTED that the largest company in the world for this market, Valve; stopped operating with Bitcoin payments on its Steam platform, because of the variations of the cryptocurrency and the increase in commissions; ensuring that in the near future they will resume the payment system, which they described as effective, safe, fast and timely.

HOWEVER, there are hundreds of companies that currently use this billing method:

STEAM:
A virtual platform for online games that has millions of registered users, promotes Bitcoin as one of its accepted cryptocurrencies.

JOLTFUN:
Through the websites of this renowned company it is easy, fast and simple to use your virtual Bitcoin wallet to buy the games of your choice.

G2A:
Digital store for the sale of video games through multiplatform

codes, which is on the list of the most important in the world, has among its payment methods; operations with Bitcoin.

BITREFILL:

This company's website is a great opportunity for video game fans, as it offers you to buy cards and pay balance in electronic game stores and thus, access these in a simple and practical way. In addition, Bitrefill provides its customers with technical support for instant payments using Lightning Network.

Instant-Gaming:

Specialized in the sale of codes for electronic games for a variety of platforms, it supports Bitcoin as one of its payment formats.

IT AND ELECTRONICS:

WITHIN THE MULTIPLE productive sectors of the world economy that have placed great confidence in the market and digital technologies, giving outstanding and preponderant position to the billing systems through Bitcoins and that makes it figure in a position of great relevance; is the computer and electronics industry, considering its great dynamics, constant variants and novel technologies. It seems that both, the IT industry and cryptocurrencies, travel hand in hand.

Below is a brief list of those companies associated with the Bitcoin payment system.

MICROSOFT:

Although the mode of payment with Bitcoins is not available worldwide, for the United States this company opens the doors to payments with this cryptocurrency, through which various licenses, equipment, memberships and other services can be purchased.

HOSTINGER:

Website that promotes, offers and provides services for the purchase of hosting, domains and the most recognized virtual servers in the world; operates payments with Bitcoin in its billing platforms.

EXPRESSVPN:

Company specialized in the sale of VPN services for more and greater privacy on the internet for users seeking to maintain their presence on reserve through the web; they acquire their services by paying for them also in Bitcoin mode.

WORDPRESS:

The largest blogging platform in the world is one of those that joins this cryptographic form of buying and selling.

NAMECHEAP:

Company specialized in web hosting services, digital and cybersecurity, domain names (DNS) and other services, with extensive and recognized trajectory, saw in this cryptocurrency; an opportunity to expand its range of action.

So, the list is too long to detail each and every one of the commercial and production areas such as industries, companies and health organizations, prevention, food production, manufacturing, real estate services, communications, transportation, etc., that have incorporated in their buying and selling platforms the secure and guaranteed Bitcoin system as an important tool and resource with facilitating prestige in their transactions. There is no doubt that all of the above, totally verifiable, represents for the Bitcoin cryptocurrency, a wonderful letter of introduction for its growth and expansion.

TRANSACTIONS

Sending or transferring economic funds or value between two parties. For Bitcoin these transactions represent records that will be stored in its Blockchain system.

Transactions represent a secure and simple way to use digital money under various platforms, electronic payments are a complete for the modern economy.

THE ENVIRONMENT where the movement and effective functioning of cryptocurrencies is accommodated, is in the transactions, which represent the operational core of the system for digital payments; opening the range of options to use fast, easy and safe money in reliable operations.

Bitcoin transactions are safe, protected and trustworthy; counting with an advanced technological structure and offering monitoring as well as training and education to its users or subscribers. The electronic transport of digital money through Bitcoin is part of an activity that is meticulously and tactfully taken care of to provide peace of mind and support at all times.

IN BITCOIN, transactions are translated as the sending of cryptocurrencies between two people through the network, and as already mentioned; their records are archived or stored in the Blockchain, block chain. Now, in order to have the option to make a transaction, there must be a resource that allows it; we refer then to a digital purse or wallet, from which we can manage and handle our funds or cryptocurrencies. Digital purses or wallets are software elements that facilitate the transfer of funds that will have their origin in the Blockchain or blockchain.

A BITCOIN TRANSACTION complies with a certain and determined protocol, through a thorough technological process made up of elements that guarantee security, protection and effectiveness.

INPUTS: Inputs are basic references that represent a past transaction that has not been processed in another transaction. The inputs facilitate the verification and ratification of the origin of the funds to be used in a future transaction. There, in the inputs, is the address of origin of Bitcoins.

OUTPUTS: Outputs are the ones that have the basic information of the sending address and the amount that was transferred. They also contain all the return or exchange addresses to which the returns of such transactions are sent, considering that in a single transaction there may be several outputs.

IDENTIFIER: The identifier or TXid, is unique and is not repeated, since it is the one that allows to give its own and exclusive personality to a particular transaction within the blockchain system. This is what we call the hash of each transaction.

COMMISSION FEE: The commission fee is the payment for fees or services that a miner receives after processing a transaction. For each block that is generated by a miner, Bitcoin will also generate a commission or fee in favor of the miner, all of which is moved for each successfully processed transaction of the block created.

. . .

THE MINER who has generated a new block after a completed transaction, does not receive the commission explicitly nor is it conjugated with any output, because it is not known who will be the miner benefiting from such fee. Bitcoin will leave a specific amount unlinked to any output, which will be interpreted as a commission for the miners.

THE ADVANTAGES of transacting with Bitcoin translate into:

SPEED: Compared to the traditional financial system; which after hours or even days of processing, would give its users an answer; with Bitcoin this process is immediate and cheaper.

IRREVERSIBILITY: Once a transaction is made and added to the block chain, it is practically impossible to reverse it. In addition, after a transaction is made, there is no way to cancel or refund it, which represents an advantage for several sectors of the economy and finance.

SECURITY: Always in favor of Bitcoin, since its operations are carried out through public addresses and private access keys, allowing users to freely dispose of their funds and receive payments, securely and without any type of risk.

CHEAPER COMMISSIONS: Since the fees to be paid to the miners for the generation of blocks are really low, this if we compare it with traditional banking, where the commissions for the use of channels and consultations are high and are increasing along with the inflation that takes place.

· · ·

TRANSACTIONS IN CRYPTOCURRENCIES and very punctually in Bitcoin, only represent a few cents, since these are not proportional to the amount of the transaction made, but according to the size of the same; in this way the user will see a substantial return for each movement made with their digital money, regardless of the amount of operations, consultations, transactions and other activity carried out on the platform.

Reserve of value The most recent economic and financial indicators are taking for granted that Bitcoin has been positioning itself as a very important reserve of value in the world, leaving aside gold as the main safe haven asset.

AS WE HAVE SEEN and can verify, Bitcoin continues to gain ground now in an area that is worrying for many; because among institutional investors, the fact that the cryptocurrency has represented a decrease in volatility with respect to gold, something really unprecedented and that does not cease to surprise analysts, arouses total interest. We are talking about digital money that surpasses the position of gold as a store of value.

This fact may well cause an immense adoption and widespread acceptance of Bitcoin as a financial reserve fund. All this is based on the fact that Bitcoin has been outperforming gold since mid-2020.

MANY ECONOMIC EXPERTS and financial analysts have argued that this trend could turn Bitcoin around and ultimately make it a preferred safe haven for investors as the digital gold narrative gains traction.

IT IS important to mention that, at the beginning of 2021, specifically for the first days of February, Bloomberg strategist Mike McGlone stated that the world's number one cryptocurrency would quickly reach a value of $50,000USD per BTC, as a large number of investors converted their gold funds into Bitcoin. By mid-month the predicted figure was reached.

FOR ALL BITCOINERS, active users of the cryptocurrency, the medium-term outlook is quite optimistic and encouraging. They have seen a significant growth in the value of the currency day after day, and added to this; the projections of experts, who claim that by 2022 Bitcoin will be quoted at $ 170,000 USD per unit, before consolidating as digital gold. Intensely enthusiastic news, studies and statements.

There is a virtual safe-haven battle between gold and Bitcoin, with the latter coming out strongly favored.

THE NUMBERS and quotes prove it:

CURRENTLY, the value of BTC is trading above $59,000USD, while 1oz of 10k gold has shown a decline, trading at $727.33USD.

FOR MANY PEOPLE, experts and connoisseurs in the field of digital money, it is valid and even acceptable the idea and consideration of positioning cryptocurrencies, especially Bitcoin, as an important store of value, which; and as we have seen, could even replace gold in the not too distant future, supported by the fact that the cryptocurrency is not regulated or under the condition of any entity or government.

A STORE of value is the great opportunity that one has so that the money does not suffer the imminent attacks and attacks that we see daily product of deflation and inflation of the currency, it is a way to safeguard a patrimony. Gold and Bitcoin are the two best examples of and assets most commonly used as stores of value, as it is projected that if the economy collapses, they will stand their ground.

Bitcoin Halving

Besides being the world's first digital currency, it has also implemented, thanks to an outstanding state-of-the-art technology; relevant programs and operating systems that have even been adopted by other cryptocurrency services; we are making direct reference to halving, which is more than a structural procedure; it is an important resource in which the block gain of a cryptocurrency is fragmented into two exactly equal parts with the firm purpose of minimizing its issuance level.

Since then halving figures as one of the most important processes within the Bitcoin economic procedure.

Bitcoin halving is a computerized process that was created as a resource to stimulate mining through Proof of Work.

Bitcoin launched its halving process, considering that the number of Bitcoins that could exist will become finite and the configuration of its software is determined only for exactly 21 million cryptocurrencies.

The software is designed to release the Bitcoins and thus reward the miners, while creating blocks and validating transactions, as we have already indicated; every 10 minutes. Halving is a process that is always active and does not stop, the amount of Bitcoins to be released is never the same, it is indeterminate, as the software is designed to halve a number of blocks every certain amount of time.

The process is also designed to determine a time until the issuance of cryptocurrencies has been completed and thus achieve a deflationary model and make the value of Bitcoin increase progressively. This process runs strictly automatically, as it was set up and is configured in its internal processing code, no patterns or anything similar, the process will run as such.

It is not programmed how often a halving will occur, it is unpredictable and incalculable when a block will be mined. What is feasible is that by means of a historical average and looking at mining reports, an average computation can be made to estimate that moment.

Bitcoin halving occurs every 210,000 blocks, considering that the network average is every 10Min. So a halving can occur every 4 years, like this:

We multiply the 210,000 blocks by 10 minutes, average block creation time. We obtain 2,100,000 and divide by 60 minutes, result: 35,000 hours, divided by 24 (1 day) = 1,458.333 days and divide again by 365 (days that represent a year) = 3.995 years A halving occurs on average, every 4 years.

THE NEXT HALVING EVENT, according to historical calculations and the previous ones occurred on November 28, 2012, July 09, 2016 and May 22, 2020; would occur on May 5, 2024 at 07:06HRS UTC.

WHEN A RESOURCE or tool stands out for its versatility, effectiveness, productivity, security and trust; it becomes an advanced instrument and this very prestige will force it to be better every day.

Bitcoin Halving resulted in that, the referential and useful tool for the world cryptographic system, where most of the cryptocurrencies adopted it and took it for themselves. All to the benefit of the global participants within the system.

BITCOIN FORKS and why you should not invest in them In the world of programming and computer science, forks are understood as the modification of code that is made to a free software. A forked code is usually very similar to the original, only that it has important modifications, however, both versions of software can be compatible.

IN CERTAIN OR certain occasions a fork is used as a testing resource for a software, however; in the field of cryptocurrencies, these forks are used to establish important system changes or to create a new currency with similar characteristics and very similar to the genuine one.

WHEN THE SAME cryptocurrency is split in two, an event known as Hard Fork (there is also the Soft Fork that we will explain in a simple way) or Hard Fork occurs. In this process, the existing code of the cryptocurrency to be copied is changed, resulting in two "similar" versions of the same coin. We will then have as a result of Hard Fork, a new coin taken from an original or old one. Two coins of the same specimen.

LET'S CONSIDER:

SOFT FORK: The process in which the two versions of the same software are compatible with each other.

HARD FORK: this process the two versions of the same software are incompatible.

AS WE CAN UNDERSTAND, both types of forks result in two different versions of the same software and in turn, two unequal versions of blockchain and two unequal versions of token or coins, but a Hard

Fork seeks to create two incompatible blockchains or coins, while a Soft Fork produces two compatible versions of token and software.

AN INTERESTING EXAMPLE of a Bitcoin Soft Fork is SegWit, which was designed to create two compatible versions of the same software by sharing a single coin. Both the original and the replicated SegWit software use the same Bitcoin.

BITCOIN CASH

PRODUCT OF A HARD FORK, Bitcoin aimed its creation process to consolidate this new currency as a different asset with a different value. After this event, Bitcoin and Bitcoin Cash became two perfectly different virtual currencies, so much so that it is impossible to transfer Bitcoin Cash (BCH) to the Bitcoin Blockchain (BTC) and vice versa, as their chains are not compatible.

BITCOIN SV

BITCOIN SATOSHI'S VERSION, Bitcoin SV (BSV). Supported by the Peer-To-Peer network, it is a currency that arose as part of the projects resulting from the genuine Bitcoin (BTC) code, making its way from a fork in the blockchain, from another forked currency, Bitcoin Cash (BCH). Despite being a project taken from Bitcoin (BTC), it has primary modifications that modify the methodology for its mining and data storage in its blockchain. Bitcoin SV, like Bitcoin (BTC), is also a decentralized digital currency useful for business, operations and transactions in the virtual network.

. . .

IT IS important to note that not all Hard Fork processes, and not always, proceed to originate a new virtual currency with its own value, they can also be created as a software update, resulting in another currency or token.

WHY NOT INVEST IN THEM?

EVERY MARKET INVESTMENT has its risks, both in traditional negotiations and those of new digital trends, and investment in cryptocurrencies does not escape this controversy. Since the appearance of the first digital currency or cryptocurrency in the world, when Bitcoin (BTC) saw the light, many began to appear, some failed to keep others are still as active and productive with Bitcoin (BTC) and from which emerged, through a process of bifurcation the two seen above:

Bitcoin Cash (BCH) and Bitcoin SV (BSV).

Without discussion, Bitcoin (BTC) remains the leader in the world of virtual currencies, growing to such an extent that it is already seen as a reserve of value that is believed to surpass gold, perhaps this is one of the reasons for its unstoppable growth.

BUT WHY NOT INVEST IN Bitcoin Cash (BCH) and Bitcoin SV (BSV)?

JUST A FEW BRIEF aspects and then dear reader, consider your own conclusions:

BITCOIN CASH (BCH)

turns out to be like a new version of Microsoft Word, which allows you to generate documents with fantastic new features but which can no longer be opened or viewed through the previous versions.

. . .

MANY CRITICS AND ANALYSTS, specialized in the field consider Bitcoin Cash (BCH) to be an overly centralized currency and that a huge handful of miners make most of the coins.

-

BITCOIN CASH (BCH) and Bitcoin SV (BSV), tend to be a fork conceived and created as part of a radical and controversial philosophy. Consequently, and for that reason they are considered and valued as high-risk cryptographic investment tools or instruments.

- ALTHOUGH THE BITCOIN SV team claims to have efficient developments, operations are susceptible to vulnerability in the network due to double spending.

- IT USES the name and brand 'Bitcoin' to gain popularity, but it does not really offer revolutionary or positive elements.

THE PRICE **of Bitcoin**

IT HAS BEEN EXPOSED several times in the course of this work, however, let's review and remember that Bitcoin is a decentralized digital financial system, since it does not belong to any government or company that regulates it and it is not considered legal currency in any country. All its operations and transactions are digital and traded through cryptocurrencies. Bitcoin is a currency every day stronger, more powerful and a store of value with great financial expectations around the world.

. . .

How is the price of Bitcoin determined, why does it go up and down every second?

THE PRICE of Bitcoin is determined by those who wish to participate in its buying and selling transaction, i.e., its subscribers and users who make life on this digital money platform. Regardless of the dynamics and constant financial movements, its value will always be set by its users.

THE ECONOMIC ACTIVITY of which Bitcoin is a participant offers the possibility of being freely distributed and benefiting from it. Bitcoin producers, the miners, have the facility to propose a price for the cryptocurrency when offering it for sale to interested parties and thus reach a mutual agreement. Between them they will make value proposals setting out a price with the idea that the other person will accept it, so that, between haggling and back-and-forth, they end up accepting an amount that satisfies the parties involved.

We can do our business over the phone or sitting over coffee, but in a totally globalized and digital world, it is more practical, safe and common to see these negotiations in online environments, optimized and specialized in cryptoassets; the well-known Bitcoin trading platforms, where the person interested in the sale can publish his proposal at a desired price.

THE PRICE of Bitcoin tends to vary or fluctuate at every moment, just like any other type of product. The value of the dollar, the euro, the pound, etc., also varies, it is enough to just take a look at any indicator to check it. The same dynamic that our society lives makes the same fluctuation movement. Everything goes up and everything goes down.

. . .

IT IS clear that there is no single platform in the world dedicated to the exclusive trading of cryptocurrencies, especially for Bitcoin, there are many that offer these supply and demand services, each one having its own operating conditions and negotiation policies that will be accepted by the interested parties that generate the movement-value of the cryptocurrency.

Regardless of such market characteristics, they all tend to seek a point of equilibrium and more or less equal value. When there are very noticeable differences between two related products or elements, the consumer public, buyer or investor, will opt to negotiate for the cheaper one and then sell on the reference of the more expensive one. This happens all the time and can be seen, as mentioned above, in the free consultation indicators on the web. This is called free arbitrage of sale, seeking to give uniformity to the prices on the various value exchange platforms.

WHY IS IT DEFLATIONARY?

One of the most important points is that Bitcoin is deflationary by nature and there are two essential rules that will give us the answer to this characteristic of value in the cryptocurrency.

1.- BITCOIN WILL ONLY ISSUE 21 million coins.

2.- ARITHMETICALLY, every four years on average there is a 50% reduction in the Bitcoin commissions received by miners for block validation, known as halving.

IN ADDITION to these two basic and well-known aspects, there is the hoarding or retention by users, which will continue to increase its value.

. . .

THE LIMITATION in the production of cryptocurrencies, i.e., the amount of Bitcoins that will exist, is the first major factor of interest that will influence the cryptocurrency to increase its price together with the halving process. These two aspects induce that the amount of total digital coins to be printed and distributed is finite and that the release of coins occurs every quarter years.

THIS DEMONSTRATES the transparency of the processes which results in an increase in value every 10 minutes and with it, the fact that every day there are less and less coins that will be in the hands of the market. A very clear evidence of Bitcoin deflation.

Bitcoin vs. FIAT Money

HAVING today so that it is greater and having today that which tends to devalue. We can translate it as in owning Bitcoins has increased in value and having funds in dollars or euros that in themselves will lose value day by day.

Bitcoin was born to stay, and with it a very well delimited fringe that stands firm and separates money from governments.

A PHENOMENON that is often striking and interesting is what happens and is evidenced when certain socio-cultural movements go public and declare themselves Anti-State and against any political or partisan current. Something like this is what happens with the deflationary character of Bitcoin and its relevant positioning in the cryptographic market against the traditional economy and the current traditional money circulating printed and produced by decree of its rulers who give it legal institutional course, fiat money.

· · ·

IN FRONT of fiat money that is issued and printed by governmental decrees and order, centralized, without backing and representation that together with other related currencies lives a constant process of devaluation that in turn generates inflation in their own economies, there is Bitcoin a cryptocurrency; fundamentally and definitely the introduction and spearhead of a global financial system of transfers represented by a credible and neutral open source value without permission requirements, decentralized; also cryptographically secure, truthful and reliable.

THIS THRIVING CRYPTO-ECONOMY, recognized and accepted by over 100 million users and still in its infancy, relatively very young and only 11 years old in the digital marketplace, has essentially transformed the message of what money itself could be in the present and perhaps what it could become in the future.

BITCOIN'S THIRD HALVING, recorded in May 2020, generated a 50% reduction in Bitcoin block fees awarded to miners who are charged with ensuring transaction validation and securing the network. This event represents a notable distinction between the monetary systems established by decree or law in the hands of governments, banks and institutions and the emerging cryptographic system executed by means of software and technological programs. In view of the world economic crisis we are currently facing, developing a technological monetary system is an opportunity to reactivate productive sectors at all levels.

THE UNLIMITED CAPACITY of states to print their money in today's world operates in stark contrast to Bitcoin, gradually decreasing issuance through an immutable monetary policy. The halving of Bitcoin in the context of the pandemic provided an appealing starting

point to discuss the central difference between the fiat and cryptocurrency money paradigms and the distribution of power in both.

STORING your Bitcoins

BITCOIN, like other cryptocurrencies, is part of the Pee-To-Peer (P2P)
payment network, which is totally free and decentralized. This means
that there are no external mediators or controllers such as banks to
register as a user in a new account. The interested party can do this
process directly, free of charge, online and in real time, and can open
as many accounts as he/she wishes, there are no limits. These
accounts are called addresses and each address is in conjunction with
a password or private key that allows to certify who is its owner and
to verify the funds in its possession.

THE FUNDS STORED in these addresses are controlled thanks to the
existence of the well-known cryptocurrency wallets. The wallets are
actually special software that allow to manage and monitor the
accounts, funds, movements and status of cryptocurrencies. These
cryptocurrency wallets allow users to send and receive payments
from anywhere in the world at any time.

THANKS TO THESE WALLETS, the owners are allowed to store their
digital currencies in a safe and simple way. Precisely for that purpose
and for that purpose they were created. Although there are countless
options, all wallets have one thing in common: they are an expeditious way to use cryptocurrencies.

CRYPTOCURRENCIES HAVE A VERY similar operation to the Zelle digital
payment system, in which your email address is the exclusive identi-

fier to recognize you as the sole owner of the account. Your address is valid to receive payments and also to make them in favor of another person, using the recipient's email address that identifies him/her as such.

In the case of cryptocurrencies such as Bitcoin, instead of using your email address, the user is assigned a unique, special and unrepeatable address. Let's see an example of a real Bitcoin user address:

1A1zP1eP5QGefi2DMPTfTL5SLmv7DivfNa (THE WALLET address of Satoshi Nakamoto back in 2009, to this day many people continue to send him some BTC, satoshis, in the form of thanks for having created the Bitcoin).

THESE ADDRESSES ARE LINKED to a mathematically related key in conjunction with a private key that is generated when the wallet is initiated. The creation is almost infinite and secure, which is a great advantage and support to keep your account in total reserve.

Cryptocurrency wallets are software, through which Bitcoin allows users to save their funds, manage them and from there, under a strict technical support of advanced technology, security and privacy; make transactions and payments freely, without intermediaries, from anywhere in the world and via internet from a computer or mobile device.

When it comes to the safety and security of our cryptocurrency funds, we know that it is not a game and we should not take it lightly. For this imperative reason hard wallets were created; physical devices designed to provide the greatest possible security and protection to funds and digital money constantly.

HARD WALLETS, as mentioned before, are physical devices which are activated in the same way as a digital wallet, but without the need to be connected to the Internet, keeping inside them in a secure and reserved way the storage of private keys. These Hard Wallets are part of the known Cold Wallets, whose name is due to the cold working condition, because they do not need to be connected to the internet or to a Blockchain, which makes them of exceptional condition.

THEY ARE SPECIALLY DESIGNED devices with the purpose of providing security at all times. In small physical formats (similar to a pendrive), these HSM (Hardware Security Modules) units with a military scale security level, access the creation of private keys that will always be kept there, in the security device.

If a hardware wallet is physically tampered with fraudulently with the intention of accessing the keys, it "commits suicide", leaving the device blank.

Hard wallets are one of the safest, most convenient and guaranteed options on the market when it comes to private storage for large amounts of cold cryptocurrencies. All this is due to the protection of the private keys inside, allowing a very convenient use, usually via USB; easy to transport and store.

Using a type of high security chip, these devices store all the keys, which once entered cannot be copied to any computer or transferred out of it.

The basic functions of hard wallets are to generate private keys and to sign with those keys the content that is assigned to them. Thus, the private key never leaves the device, it will always be there, protected.

LEDGER

LEDGER IS a technology company specialized in the development of infrastructure and security solutions for cryptocurrencies and Blockchain. Among the flagship designs offered to the market are the Ledger Nano S and Ledger Nano X.

. . .

LEDGER NANO S:

It is one of the most recommended digital wallets for cryptocurrencies in the crypto industry. Ledger Nano S is the suggested digital device for storing Bitcoins. It is a hardware that allows storing different types of digital currencies in the most secure and guaranteed way.

LEDGER NANO X:

It is the most recent device manufactured and offered by the Ledger company. It has been designed and configured with the most secure and mobile hardware in the cryptocurrency world. Cold bluetooth wireless connection, it will support users to process their digital funds on the move.

TREZOR:

LIKE LEDGER, Trezor is also a technology solutions developer and creator of the first physical wallets with a formidable reputation in the IT and security industry. Trezor wallets are also physical devices capable of providing secure storage of cryptographic private keys. They are also deterministic wallets (HD), since they have the ability to generate unlimited addresses from the original one.

Its operating system is compatible with Android, Windows, OSX and Linux, once configured for the first time, it displays on its home screen, what is known as "seed" with 24 keywords from an RNG, also cold and without internet connection. It is important to note that the seed will never be outside the device, so Trezor will create a solitary environment to trigger the signing of off-line transactions. A totally secure way that will not allow the user's password to be discovered.

. . .

IN OTHER VERSIONS of this same company, there are: Trezor One and Trezor T.

These devices are manufactured in a friendly design and have a user interface easy and simple to use, supporting the entry for a very large number of cryptocurrencies.

THE KEYS of your cryptocurrencies

WITH ALL THIS accelerated and galloping growth of today's technology, it is often more difficult to keep our privacy intact. Let's think for a moment about big name companies and the high level of work they put into keeping all their data safe and secure.

THE WORLD of cryptocurrencies does not escape from this situation and is in search of guaranteed security and privacy, often the users themselves become their own guardians and agents for the protection of their identity. Fortunately, there are many technology companies worldwide that are dedicated to researching, developing and activating hardware, software and operating systems adapted to every need with the sole purpose of guaranteeing what people want so badly:

PRIVACY AND CRYPTOGRAPHIC SECURITY.

WHY KEEP THE KEYS?

ALL PEOPLE active in the online environment and especially those who handle money digitally, are definitely obliged to keep their identity in total privacy and security, so that, for example, only the owner of a crypto-asset account can be the only one to have full control over it.

There is no doubt that we all need to have a secure and private identity, our names, numbers, passwords and other data do not want to be shared with an open external community. Whoever ventures into the digital ecosystem is obliged to keep their keys and general information of this newly created environment in total reserve, only then will be able to perform all transactions and offer services, with security and anonymity guaranteed. It is therefore convenient to have a private data storage, so there will be no way for personal and financial information to be filtered and exported by and to third parties. All this will allow the user to participate in smooth, personalized and secure processes with complete peace of mind.

BUYING and selling Bitcoin

IN THE CRYPTOGRAPHIC network there is a fantastic condition and modality of service that keeps the platform active 24 hours a day, 365 days a year, and that possibility of buying and selling Bitcoin to the highest bidder at the right place and time, from any place or geographical point in the world, regardless of the time and with just one click from your computer or device through an internet connection.

This constant movement is what has maintained and keeps Bitcoin active since its appearance and from that famous transaction to buy and pay for two pizzas, that day; in 10,000BTC. Well, its safe and reliable activity, its great trajectory and unquestionable acceptance, has generated until today, a little more than a hundred users; and it is still growing.

Having fiat money available to be immediately exchanged for Bitcoins has resulted in an unquestionably profitable negotiation. A clear example of this can be seen in those who in 2010 converted 100$USD into Bitcoins at the price of 0.003 cents, today would have in his wallet the equivalent of 73,000,000$USD. He would be a millionaire! Something surprising and unimaginable. This is how this formidable cryptocurrency has been working and growing.

To ENTER into negotiations with digital money that allow the purchase and sale of cryptoassets, it is necessary to have an account and its respective digital wallet, in addition to the funds available to bid for the future transaction. There is a giant menu of digital platforms, specialists in the field and with all the resources required for such purposes, which provide users with guidance, training and education, before deciding to process the sending of their money to a recipient, either to make a payment or to make the purchase of a product, good or service.

These digital platforms dedicated to the processing of transactions and various cryptographic operations, must have and comply with all a series of protocols necessary to ensure basic and fundamental security, confidentiality and privacy that also provide confidence and protection to the user who will circulate their funds through the web through its servers.

As has been said, there are many options, many alternatives, many from which to choose the one we consider to be the best according to our criteria and subjectivity. It is an online, globalized world in which direct and traditional personal contact is not the main tool. It is recommended to be careful and cautious to have peace of mind and know that your cryptocurrencies are very well protected and there, available and usable for when it is time to make any movement with them or the next transaction. Knowing that everything is safe and running smoothly when we are, especially; buying and selling Bitcoins.

Now, is there any special platform to perform these operations, is any platform safe, can we process funds with more than one? Let's see below a brief detail of some alternatives that have earned the prestige and trust of an important number of Bitcoiners.

. . .

BUYING on Coinbase

ONE OF THE MOST SECURE, reliable and popular platforms in the world for the purchase of Bitcoins, besides being simple, practical and friendly navigation. Coinbase so far remains one of the most reliable on the web.

This website is the most popular one on the market. It is very fast and easy to use. Through Coinbase you can make the purchase of Bitcoins by means of a credit card or a bank transfer. The administrative costs for commission vary according to the service to be used and geographic region, however, they are really very low and attractive costs for the customer.

Coinbase offers totally free services to its customers such as:

Cryptocurrency safekeeping Since Coinbase also offers the wallet service, associated to its Exchange list, the client will not have to pay for acquiring the wallet nor for its maintenance.

Transfers between internal wallets in Coinbase There is no commission charge for transfers and operations from one Coinbase wallet to another, i.e. between the same customers; this being a very usual procedure, it is free and exempt from any operational charge.

Coinbase Commerce Service Designed especially for customers who own a business, Coinbase has created its Coinbase Commerce product as an extension of Exchange that allows its merchant customers to accept payments in their business with cryptocurrencies, for which no commission charges are made, it is a free service Other Coinbase services with fees or commissions:

THE PLATFORM ASSIGNS two commission systems. The first is a spread (a difference that is added to the final price of the asset within the market) and the second is the fixed or percentage commission made to the operation and which is variable according to the amount.

· · ·

BUYING and selling cryptocurrencies with Fiat Money

THE PLATFORM CHARGES a commission or Spread charge on the closing value of the asset in the market of 0.50% of the price. It should be noted that this percentage amount is not fixed, as Coinbase makes its customers aware by warning that this Spread is variable according to their daily mobility in the market.

In conjunction with the Spread, the platform charges a commission that may vary as a fixed percentage or according to the amount of the operation and subject to change according to the geographical location from where the client is performing the operation. Coinbase in all its operations will always charge the higher of the fixed and the variable percentage.

Conversion of cryptocurrency for another cryptocurrency From its platform, Coinbase charges these transactions by means of Spreads on the prices of the cryptocurrencies to be converted. The Spread has the rate of 1% on the price of the cryptocurrency to be acquired. Coinbase will always let its clients know that the percentage of the Spread could vary according to the movements and activity of the market.

BUYING Coinbase Bundle

THE COINBASE PLATFORM provides the Coinbase Bundle service to purchase multiple digital currencies from a single transaction. The advantage of this offer is that Coinbase will not charge any commission for each cryptocurrency, but will make a general charge for the purchase and lump sum as if it were a single purchase. The commission that is charged by Coinbase Bundle is equal to that charged for making a single asset purchase.

. . .

BUYING on Changelly

AVAILABLE TO ALL users who are looking for an effective way to manage their digital currencies, the website offers this platform, considered one of the fastest on the web to exchange cryptocurrencies securely, through bank cards or fund transfers. Through Changelly you have the opportunity to buy Bitcoins among the most known and used cryptocurrencies.

Among its basic purposes or objectives, Changelly has proposed to break with the large number of schemes and paradigms in technical and administrative barriers to the new trend of the digital market, providing the possibility of acquiring cryptocurrencies with the sole use of other cryptocurrencies as a resource or payment element, through minimum commission costs for the provision of its services.

This platform offers in a very particular way the opportunity to buy or sell digital currencies in a fast and safe way. This means that there are no charting tools, order books or anything similar.

CHANGELLY IN ADDITION to operating as an exchange house, also offers products and online services with attention and guidance from its website, wallet service and payment processors to receive cryptocurrencies at the best market rate to both individuals and companies that receive this modality, a widget service for customers to incorporate the platform into their websites and trade with a total of 52 virtual currencies.

CHANGELLY COMMISSIONS

PURCHASES MADE on the platform are subject to a price offered by Changelly, which is above the market value. For the reverse process, the sale from the platform will reflect a bid price that is below market value. Profit or discount margins are usually not reflected or published.

A MATHEMATICAL CALCULATION performed by the firm Cryptowisser, based on an activity on December 9, 2020, compared the prices offered by Changelly against Coinmarketcap.com. The comparison showed that, on a percentage average, Changelly's prices were higher/lower by 0.86% than those offered by Coinmarketcap. It is therefore, and as many claim; one of the best crypto platforms and alternatives with the most attractive trading fees.

BUYING with CEX.IO

CEX.IO IS a leading crypto asset management services platform known in the cryptocurrency industry and is one of the longest running Bitcoin exchanges. CEX.IO covers an extensive range of crypto services offered from its multifunctional platform for payment methods, security and legal issues.

Through CEX.IO it is possible to buy, sell and trade various cryptocurrencies including Bitcoin (BTC), Litecoin (LTC) and Ethereum (ETH) for traditional money. With a technology developed to meet the requirements of beginners and experts in trading; CEX.IO offers excellent solutions, among which stand out; having a simplified buying interface and cross-platform trading through its website, provision of a mobile application and APIs. With CEX.IO it is guaranteed and safe to safeguard the funds in the account, thanks to its storage service.

As in other digital platforms, everything starts from the moment you proceed to open a completely free account from its web portal, responding to each and every one of the requirements requested there. Once you have created your new account for crypto-assets management, it is advisable to enable the authentication process through the phone or through the Google Authenticator application to maintain the security of your account and your funds that from now on you will manage with CEX.IO.

As part of the system, the user will have state-of-the-art technological resources to control the purchase, exchange and management of virtual currencies through the wallet provided by the application. This wallet allocation is free of charge and there is no charge for it.

CEX.IO has a feature for its services that results in something very particular, and that is that in favor of the client it offers in its web portal the physical address of its offices in London (United Kingdom). This detail does not mean that it is more secure just because of a location, but those in the know are sure that it is an aspect that provides a lot of confidence among its distinguished portfolio of clients.

To this point we add another highlight, and that is that they publish a phone number for personalized attention from the United Kingdom and from the United States and to complement, three email addresses for support, assistance and technical support, in addition to their social networks on Twitter, Telegram and Facebook. CEX.IO, thinking about the best way to reach and capture an audience eager to be part of the cryptographic spectrum, opens all the communication channels currently available.

One of its flagship services is trading, an exchange that facilitates spot and margin trading.

When the trading service is performed on spot, it is operated from its standard platform, and when it is on margin, it is necessary to work from the broker.cex.io page, where the trading service offered is much more advanced and from which it is also possible to perform spot operations.

CEX.IO OFFERS OTHER SERVICES:

IT PROVIDES the possibility to buy cryptocurrencies paid via VISA and Mastercard credit cards in four currencies, namely; US dollars, euros, pound sterling, ruble.

PURCHASES CAN BE MADE from the CEX.IO web platform or via the application that can be downloaded from Google Play or App Store Trading can also be performed from the mobile application.

Staking, a financing service whereby users activate a crypto-work program to generate extra expenses using their wallets.

THE LENDING SERVICE with CEX.IO where the alternative of borrowing classic currencies such as Bitcoin or Ethereum is given.

CEX.IO and its commissions

EVERY TRADE IS between two parties: the originator, whose order will be in the order book prior to the trade, and the taker, who places the order in line with the originator's order. The originators generate liquidity in favor of the market and the takers take it away when both orders coincide.

Commissions for CEX.io operations apply at 0.25% for takers. This commission rate is on par with the market average. The exchange industry provides a discount of 0.16% to originators, the margin through which they operate their transactions. This results in a profit for investors with no interest in taking existing orders from the book.

As THE TRADER increases the levels of their trades, commissions are reduced, which can be as low as 0.10% for takers and 0.00% for originators.

There are a plethora of options, alternatives and offerings of active exchanges and crypto services that are at the click of a button, delivered to offer the best in a comprehensive manner. These platforms will continue to flourish as time goes by, and in proportion to the growth of demand and birth of new cryptocurrencies, as in tune with the obligation to satisfy the needs of the society that day by day joins this digital money trend.

We HAVE MENTIONED ONLY THREE: Coinbase, Changelly and CEX.io, with very brief and punctual reviews. Dear reader, we invite you to dig a little deeper and get to know them a little more beyond this reading. We open a web portal, we explore and it is up to us to register in the platform that we consider that most resembles us and offers us the best in the market. The purpose is to be calm and to make the money produce a real store of value.

Exchanges (exchange and trading platforms) In proportion to the growth of the cryptocurrency market that is expanding every day gaining more and more ground as a financial resource, new exchange houses continue to be born, a place where we can acquire the desired digital funds and start our own exchange and trading operations. With such a large number of options, it can be somewhat complicated to discern which and what is best suited to the needs of each prospect.

Hundreds exist and are active on the web, and some even make physical offices and other links such as phone lines and e-mails available to their users and potential new clients. A basic factor inspires the creation of these Exchanges and it is precisely the cryptographic environment itself that indirectly drives their appearance, another the amount of digital currencies available in the market and finally, among perhaps many more; the need to consume and own them, but above all to handle, manage and process them properly; there comes into play the Exchange of your choice.

COINBASE

IT IS a web portal specialized in the area of digital currency exchange that allows access to the cryptocurrency market, with a great offer available from which to choose the cryptoasset we have been looking for. It is also considered as one of the facilitating reference services for buying and selling digital currencies for experienced users as well as for those who are new to the market. Coinbase works perfectly as a virtual wallet where virtual funds are stored and managed as a viable resource for acquiring new currencies.

Coinbase is a web platform, you can manage it from the internet fulfilling two formidable functions. Use it as a digital purse or wallet where cryptocurrencies acquired can be stored with privacy and security in a single site and as your virtual bank, which you can consult to know the status of your funds, their movements and behavior, as well as their evolution in value.

The financial portal also works as a service for the purchase and sale of cryptocurrencies, being able to combine your traditional credit card with the Coinbase platform and use your fiat money to buy and pay for the virtual currency of your choice, which you can trade whenever you want or need.

Coinbase is headquartered in San Francisco, California (USA) founded in 2012 by Brian Armstrong and Fred Ehrsam. One of its main investors is BBVA through its BBVA Ventures program. By July 2019 the platform claimed to have 30 million active users.

. . .

BINANCE A DEPOSIT guarantee is a fund managed to ensure that the relationship of the parties involved is compliant. A way to secure the financial relationship. Binance is a P2P (Peer-To-Peer) Exchange, where people can conduct a secure and private business relationship. Here you can buy and sell your cryptocurrencies with your legal tender as a guarantee fund. In the process of negotiating the purchase and sale of funds, the digital coins of the seller will be placed in a temporary guarantee fund and will be retained as a deposit guarantee until the transaction is successfully completed between both parties.

Binance is undoubtedly one of the best exchanges and has been among the most popular recently. It has now gained great recognition in the crypto world due to the wide variety of currencies it offers for trading and its very low transaction fees.

Changpeng Zhao is the name of an important figure behind Binance. He is a Chinese-Canadian entrepreneur, founder of the platform that today is the largest cryptocurrency exchange in the world due to the outstanding number of transactions it registers daily, thanks to its advantages, quality of services and trust in favor of its many users who register every day.

3

WHY DID THE BLOCKCHAIN CHANGE THE WORLD AND HOW CAN YOU TAKE ADVANTAGE OF IT?

T he Bitcoin cryptocurrency and some others are usually associated directly with Blockchain.

Its origins date back to 1991, thanks to its creators Stuart Haber and W. Scott Stornetta, who unveiled the first project based on a strictly cryptographically secured blockchain.

It was not noticed more than a decade later, exactly in 2008, when, thanks to the arrival of Bitcoin, this powerful process became popular. In the contemporary history of cryptography, its use is manifesting a strong demand for its use in other commercial applications, giving Blockchain the projection towards an annual growth of 51% by

2022 in diverse markets on the web, basically that of financial institutions and internet businesses.

The blockchain, or better known as Blockchain, is a single, distributed and consensual record in several nodes of a network. For the topic of cryptocurrencies, this process would be like the ledger in which each and every movement is recorded.

THE OPERATIONAL AND functional system of Blockchain could be complex and perhaps difficult to understand if you delve into the internal details that compose it and its structural implementation.

In the following, let's see the basic idea of its activity and work.

EACH BLOCK IS responsible for storing:

- Valid records or transactions.
- Information related to the block.
- Linkage with the previous block and the contiguous block by means of the hash in each block.

THUS, each block has a precise and immovable location within the blockchain, as each block contains information from the hash of the block preceding it. A complete chain of blocks is stored in its respective node within the network to thus constitute the blockchain. Thus, upon completion, an exact copy of the chain is stored for all network participants.

As new records are created, they are initially verified and validated by the network nodes and then added to a new block that is linked to the blockchain.

· · ·

Data Storage

Consists of storing and replicating information to generate reliable historical data.

Data transmission Establishment of connections through peer-to-peer networks.

Data confirmation

Process open to the public that has the appropriate device for this case. It is competitive and transparent in order to validate the inputs known as data mining.

The first cryptocurrency that used Blockchain, was Bitcoin, and it was used to perform a decryption associated with the currency, which for the first time handled the concept of "blockchain". Hence the claim that Bitcoin is the first cryptocurrency used on the Blockchain.

"The blockchain turns out to be a complex process, but thanks to technological advances this is done by computers and depending on their capacity, mining may or may not be productive and agile for integration into the blockchain."

R. Espinosa / Authorized Network Blockchain Benefits

Among the main benefits that describe Blockchain, it is worth mentioning the following:

- Available and reliable data:

Thanks to being decentralized operating system, it is independent process that does not require mediators or third parties, in addition to not depending on any agency, company or government, which supervises it which allows all its information and data to be easily accessible and reliable.

- ACCESS TO HIGH QUALITY DATA:

Participants in a transaction have their own accurate, timely, reliable, complete and consistent data; which is essential to be able to make a sound decision.

- TRANSPARENCY AND STABILITY:

Since blockchain is a shared database, these will be available to all network users at any point in a transaction, providing the required transparency. Once this data is created, it cannot be deleted or altered.

- INTEGRITY IN THE PROCESS:

Users participating in a transaction, know and accept that everything has been conceived as required by the agreed protocol.

- SPEED AND LOW COSTS:

Blockchains are in charge of using their own potential to generate a decrease in costs and time invested for each operation, this is due to suppressing indirect costs for exchanging assets, and not operating or participating with intermediaries.

UTILITIES OF BLOCKCHAIN

BLOCKCHAIN IS a technological mechanism that is part of a strategic plan that interprets the needs of the project, identifies the level of transparency and decentralization, determines who are the members that act as nodes and establishes the appropriate Blockchain structure, defining precisely how transactions and operations are going to be.

Blockchain software will access to create projects that are distinct from each other, so the concrete set-up that is carried out will be conclusive in saying whether or not it deserves to be validated.

It is important to carefully determine who will participate in the network and how. Whether it is a private or public network, depending on the type of network, it will be necessary to carefully design its own structure of nodes and the transactions that each one can carry out and validate. Regarding web access for your users, if any, it will be prudent to analyze what will be shown to them and how it will be shown. It is not necessary for the user to know that behind the web interface he is using there is a Blockchain network.

BLOCKCHAIN's great usefulness is undoubtedly intensely surprising, reaching sectors and productive areas that many of us never dared to imagine. We will mention just some of the areas where the usefulness of Blockchain is a wonderful window to the future.

All this, thanks to the 3 main benefits that its technology offers us. A new group of events occur and expand among us in a very positive and optimal way. From the realization of smart contracts, to the creation of specific applications by productive sectors; passing through the elementary online identification. Here are some Blockchain practices that drive the sustainability of a probable better and better world.

BLOCKCHAIN AND HEALTHCARE

THERE ARE multiple applications that Blockchain can bring to the healthcare sector. Blockchain has the facility to simplify healthcare problems and contribute to the transformation that the global healthcare sector so badly needs to provide to guarantee a longer life with higher expectations.

DATA MANAGEMENT FOR SCIENTIFIC RESEARCH: By providing an absolute record orientation, all compiled data is valuable information for the field of research, with which it is feasible to benefit society by contributing to the finding of solutions; even in the face of the current pandemic.

PREVENTING THE SPREAD OF DISEASES:

BLOCKCHAIN TECHNOLOGY, is capable of enabling the fight against the spread of pathologies. Let's imagine the case of a disease that has been generated and then spread through spoiled, contaminated or improperly handled food; through Blockchain it is possible to perform a detailed traceability of the total path that the products have made in order to determine where the contagion occurred, how and the origin of the causative bacteria.

IN THIS WAY, the spread of a disease can be prevented by recalling the food in an immediate, inspected and efficient manner.

Blockchain and food production One of the most curious uses that Blockchain can provide is in the food industry. Specifically in the agricultural sector, but also applicable to many others. This blockchain technology can be implemented with great effectiveness. The tracking of consumer products from the moment of their birth or harvest, to their distribution destination.

In addition to being possible, this platform could boast a forceful and positive change for the consumption of food produced by the agricultural sector, where all participants in the production chain would have accurate information on the origin and conditions of their products. In this way, they will opt to take the most sustainable form of production.

BLOCKCHAIN and the energy sector

FOR YEARS, it has been common for a centralized energy supplier to be responsible for supplying society with electricity. This situation is and continues to change, with more and more households and companies joining efforts to generate their own energy through renewable energy systems.

THE WEAKNESS IS that although many countries have incorporated a compensation system for the deficits and surpluses of the electricity generated, it is difficult to keep a punctual and precise control.

It is at this crossroads when Blockchain appears, offering its novel technology, could create a network of homes, businesses and / or businesses, consumers in general; and thus monitor and supervise the purchase and sale of this energy.

An interesting example is what is happening in Spain, where since 2019, the companies Iberdrola, Gas Natural Fenosa and Endesa were unified in a single project called Enerchain, supported by Blockchain, and that enables in any area of Europe transactions of electricity and gas, regardless of the day and time.

BLOCKCHAIN AND MUSIC

IN THE WORLD OF MUSIC, there are countless difficulties when it comes to the marketing and distribution of music productions. From strict copyrights, to the excessive control of profits perceived by some production companies, harming the authors and composers of music.

. . .

THANKS TO BLOCKCHAIN'S FEATURES, these conflicts can be resolved with great ease. Blockchain technology provides authors with the rights to their property, as well as a control to monitor and track the path of their works, avoiding fraudulent dysfunctions and protecting themselves against piracy.

AND HOW CAN BLOCKCHAIN DO this? Through smart contracts, payment automation and by eliminating extraneous developers. All of this creates a flawless system, based on fair terms and ensuring ease of regular payments.

OTHER SECTORS in which Blockchain has made inroads, guaranteeing its effectiveness and generating satisfaction, are journalism, communications, insurance, real estate, commerce, logistics, agriculture, vineyards, banking and finance; and offering the possibility of becoming present in areas such as telecommunications, military, transportation, travel and tourism, automotive and manufacturing. The experience of those who have already incorporated it and the magnificent results they receive, will open the doors to an extensive and very broad universe to be served.

QUITE CURIOUS UTILITIES, isn't it? And to think that the vast majority of people relate the Blockchain platform only to Bitcoins and the cryptographic system. A few other applications, much more surprising, are used with this technology, managing to reduce to zero the levels of fraud in electoral voting, animal tracking in the agricultural sector or in the unique identification of diamonds.

Now, if you did not know these other uses of Blockchain, you already have a more complete knowledge of how much it can offer in favor of society.

· · ·

ICOs (Initial Coin Offerings)

ICOs are an initial coin offering, and the financing of a business project. ICOs seek in its fundamental conception to finance the birth of a new cryptocurrency, in the best Bitcoin or Ethereum style. These are virtual tokens in small quantities, with cryptographic protection, which enjoy a certain value due to their scarcity and demand. These nascent digital currencies are very useful for making payments quite cheaply and for storing value, as some markets exchange them for real money.

Through the mining process, cryptocurrencies are created over time. The miners use all their computational power for the project, which allows the system to work efficiently and therefore receive their earnings from the mined coins that appear spontaneously and randomly as well as from the commissions received when verifying the commercial transactions that take place between the users of the cryptocurrency.

When a person decides to give life to a new digital currency, several basic steps must be fulfilled. The first one is to design the currency, then implement it by means of software, and finally make this software available to the community so that the miners, who will support the activity of this new currency, can manifest themselves.

This whole process has its costs and the specific way to finance the project is through ICOs. The developers carry out prior mining in private and behind closed doors to offer the new cryptocurrency in exchange for other currencies already in circulation, such as Bitcoin, and which are also exchangeable for real legal tender.

An ICO consists of offering to a group of initial investors, the new coins in exchange for physical fiat money. Hence, it is similar to crowdfunding, since it is a free community of users who join together to finance a project by themselves, without the participation or intervention of external, centralized organizations or any kind of intermediaries.

NFTs (Non Fungible Tokens)

AT ONLY 15 years of age, Mark Cuban ventured into a market that helped him with his studies and also to obtain, over the years, a great fortune; seeing in the philatelic market the opportunity to buy stamps at 15 cents to sell them a few blocks later for $25 each. Cuban is a multimillionaire investor, owner of the NBA's Dallas Mavericks.

He was able to capture that magic of how a simple taste for collecting, gave so much value to a physical asset. Now he faithfully believes in the power of NFTs (Non Fungible Tokens), which are the digital version of stamps, art or any other tangible or intangible item to which people attach a certain value. These assets are gaining more and more ground every day and travel along with the culture in which blockchain and cryptocurrencies are absolutely integrated.

A POKÉMON TRADING card is a good example to explain in a very simple and straightforward way the trend of this new collectible stamp format, where the concept is still the same as it was a few years ago with the famous and surprising Cryptokitties fever, which in fact is still active and trading at truly absurd prices for many.

WHY DID a digital avatar of a cat fetch $115,000? Quite simply, enough people believed and considered that its price was indeed that. There is no other answer.

Inverse to what happens with cryptocurrencies, with NFTs it is not possible to make exchanges between them, so simple because there are no two NFTs that are exactly identical and that both have even the same value: your card of a crypto-token is unique, as is a virtual work of art or any other intangible asset that connects with this concept.

NFTs ARE digital assets in line with the idea that: "From what you touch and see, to what you don't touch, but you can see". We have always given value to those tangible assets that in addition to seeing, we have been able to touch, now we do it more to those assets that we see, but probably will not be able to touch. Cryptocurrencies are a pretty clear approximation of that principle, but NFTs are in a well-marked lead, infusing reservation of value to objects more aimed at collecting.

We have a very explanatory analogy between an NFT and a theater ticket. On the ticket there is detailed information on the date, time, place, value, artists, name of the play, etc. The ticket, like the NFT, is unique and personal.

The vast majority of these tokens, which can be stamps, works of art or crypto tokens; are based on the standards of the Ethereum network and its blockchain, which allows ease when making purchase and sale transactions with them.

NFTs MEET CERTAIN CHARACTERISTICS. Strangely unique and unrepeatable, non-interoperable, indivisible, indestructible, absolute ownership and finally verifiable.

We return to Mark Cuban, an absolute believer in these virtual assets. For Cuban, NFTs are the ultimate future of business, and we quote him: "This generation knows that a digital contract and the digital asset that represents a cryptoasset are a better investment than the traditional asset that you can see, touch or feel".

4

THE MOST USED INVESTMENT METHOD
IN THE BITCOIN WORLD

Bitcoin Price and Speculation.

W ho controls token prices?
One of the biggest risks to the health of the market for Bitcoin, is the effect on it of speculation by a small group of immense capital.

Speculation is a fundamental part that affected all markets with great impact. In fact, if there were no speculation about the future price of the assets we own and acquire.

We could not be sure of investing in anything at all.

.   .   .

THE DAILY MARKET movements for all financial assets and funds depend mostly on speculation. Not only speculation by investors in consideration of the future returns on their investment, but also speculation by capital that enters the market only to buy or sell, aspiring to make more profit in the shortest possible time.

THESE ARE the types of capitals that sell Bitcoin, when for example the futures contracts of the Chicago Mercantile Exchange (CME) are about to expire, all for the purpose of pulling the spot price of Bitcoin, and thus make a profit from the loss of the market; or on the contrary are the capitals that, in the middle of the bull run of a digital currency, start buying it desperately hoping to sell it in a very short time at a higher price. This generates a huge increase in demand, which pushes prices far beyond their natural growth. And thus, a subsequent increase in supply for when this capital is withdrawn.

SADLY, this is the elementary type of investment in the virtual currency market, and especially; the basic type of investment immersed in the Bitcoin market. It is frequently affected by speculative swings, which drive the price of Bitcoin up or down as it suits them.

WHAT IS the reason behind this speculation control?

SUBSTANTIALLY THE LACK of discernment that still exists in the Bitcoin market. There are so relatively few investors in the market that point to Bitcoin as a profitable asset for its value in itself. That a few large capitals are daring to shake up the whole market, because of its relative weight in the face of the rest of the community.

· · ·

BITCOIN IS EXPECTED TO RISE: And this is the speculative predisposition that seems to have no last stage in sight. On the contrary, and as long as it is not possible to achieve a total massification of Bitcoin, this cryptocurrency will be managed by the speculative market forces that it does not control.

PRECISELY FOR THIS REASON, reports such as those published by Skew Market are so important, in which a reading is made regarding the price that investors expect for Bitcoin in the year 2022. As a result, a little more than 10% of the active agents in the stock, financial and cryptographic market are beginning to estimate, disclose and expect a very high increase for the currency over the current price.

THE VALUE OF A GOOD, asset, etc. is affected by speculation not only by possible statistical projections, but also by social-cultural actions disclosed or not on the network and conceived outside it, by governmental and political situations; despite the fact that cryptocurrencies and the digital market are a free resource and distant from these scenarios.

THESE ESTIMATES REPRESENT an important consideration towards the Bitcoin price and what would be its future value. And it is very interesting that it is based on the appreciation of an important representative group of the market, especially when in these important moments for the price of Bitcoin and its community. The currency has been gaining strength, currently standing at around $50,000.00 per unit.

Y although there is no doubt that the Bitcoin could indeed reach important values progressively. The fact that for the time being, there seem to be no specific events that drive the currency, is not a reason for it to maintain its bullish character. Beyond the excitement generated by its recent growth. It could lead us to believe and think that this is a purely speculative sentiment, and therefore represents a certain level of risk to the health of the Bitcoin market itself.

WHO CONTROLS the prices of tokens?

ACCORDING TO WILLIAM MOUGAVAR, author of the book "The Business Blockchain", a token is defined as "a unit of value that an organization creates to govern its business model and give more power to its users to interact with its products, while facilitating the distribution and sharing of benefits among all its shareholders".

IN TODAY'S CRYPTO ENVIRONMENT, it would seem that issuing a new currency is a capability that appears to be beyond central banks. The case that most exemplifies this is Bitcoin, and how a virtual currency can be placed on the market from a private environment, with all the technological support offered by Blockchain, with many restrictions due to the lack of a legal framework to regulate it. Bitcoin is just the genesis of a whole revolt whose second step could well be in tokens.

A TOKEN IS ACTUALLY nothing more than a recent qualifier for a unit of value issued by a private entity. A token bears important resemblance to Bitcoin, as it has a value that is accepted by an entire community and is established on the Blockchain, and is also both a broader concept. A token is more than a currency, as it has more uses. Likewise, the vast majority of tokens are based on the Ethereum Blockchain protocol, more complete, according to experts, than the Bitcoin Blockchain.

.   .   .

THE MAIN EXCHANGES TO know the value and then trade in tokens are currently generated by exchanges, among which the most important ones are. Bithumb, AscendEX (Bitmax), Bithumb Global, and Kyber Network. However, as we have seen elsewhere, the value of cryptocurrencies, including tokens, is fundamentally based on trust, supply and demand. Since, like other digital currencies, they are decentralized and issued by a private entity and without mediators.

RISKS AND MITIGATIONS TO **be taken into account.**
  Market risks

THE RISKS of performing operations and trading through cryptocurrencies are basically related to their volatility within the market itself. Since they represent a very high risk at all times. It is very important to understand and be aware of the risks to which one is subject before undertaking or initiating an investment in cryptocurrencies. All economic and financial assets carry a high level of risk, either through the use of leverage, unethical trading techniques or the volatility of the target market itself.

Let's see which are the most common risks that we can face and which make cryptocurrencies represent a possible investment risk:

- VOLATILITY: untimely changes in the susceptibility of the market can cause unforeseen and forceful fluctuations in its price. It is not uncommon for the value of cryptocurrencies to suffer powerful and sudden drops by hundreds or even thousands of dollars.

- UNREGULATED: Cryptocurrencies are not beholden to governments or central banks, they are not regulated or supervised by anybody. However, every day and according to the dynamics we see frequently, they are attracting a lot of attention. In fact, there are concerns about whether they should be classified and considered as commodities or as virtual currencies themselves.

- SUSCEPTIBLE TO ERRORS AND CYBER-ATTACKS: There is no perfect formula or best way to avoid technical failures, human error or cyber-attacks on the network.

- SUBJECT TO BIFURCATIONS OR INTERRUPTIONS: Financial and commercial activity with transactions using cryptocurrencies as a payment resource entails many additional risks, such as hard forks and disruptions. Those who are immersed in the world of cryptoassets need to be aware of the risks they may face before trading with these products. In the case of hard forks, there is likely to be a lot of price volatility and trading may be suspended if reliable underlying market prices are not available.

THERE ARE two sides to the coin and this one we have just seen is perhaps producing a sense of alarm. Let us turn around and see what is on the other side; and in this way look for the means or resources that will allow us to mitigate these risks. Four specific aspects that have been important at a financial level are the following:

- ACCEPT RISK as a possibility inherent to network activities.

UNDERSTAND that one is part of a universal globalized community, in which the creators and participants are generally unknown.

- REDUCE RISK THROUGH CONTROL STRATEGIES.
    Monitor, supervise and check every activity, movement and trans-

action carried out on the platforms of which you are a user, safeguarding access, passwords and other entry options.

- TRANSFER it to a third party that can manage it.

It does not mean that the risk is assumed by another person, it is about seeking the necessary guidance and assistance to provide the most expeditious solutions required by experts in the field and specialists in computer risks.

- AVOID ACTIVITIES THAT GENERATE INSECURITY.

Seek all the necessary guidance from other members and users of the network who are more experienced and who know the key operational details of the services, operations and transactions, together with the complementary tools best suited to the characteristics of the account. It is all about mobilizing funds and investing with security and confidence.

- EDUCATION AND TRAINING.

Keeping up to date, updated and duly informed about news, changes, offers, services and other dynamics generated by the platform we are part of; participating in its publications, social networks and forums in order to be as updated as possible about its activities.

- EXCHANGES Not all decentralized or non-custodial exchanges are faithful to the concept of security, but they are always willing to continue offering a more secure service than centralized exchanges.

DESPITE THE FACT that a large number of centralized exchanges, all specialists in handling cryptocurrencies were victims of multiple technological attacks and hacks, which together came to an estimated amount of almost 300 million dollars during 2019, many cryptocurrency traders still stand firm by contributing significant amounts of capital in their centralized exchanges.

Although in recent years and to the present day, quantities of specialist cryptocurrency developer services operating on a decentralized basis have been and are being launched, few are the platforms that have managed to perceive significant liquidity.

Are non-custodied platforms more secure?

Erik Voorhees, CEO for the "Noncustodial" cryptocurrency exchange ShapeShift, once asserted that non-custodial exchanges are in a position to provide the market and their users with a more secure form of structure and foundation for people to trade trusted digital assets.

- Liquidity

Liquidity risk is the potential loss and inability to roll over or incur liabilities under normal conditions for a centralized financial institution, due to the prior or forced sale of assets at unusual discounts to meet certain obligations or because something cannot be sold or purchased.

Liquidity risk arises when one of the participating parties holds assets of interest, but does not have the liquidity to meet its commitments. In the event that the company cannot meet its short-term debts even if it sells its current assets, it will be in a situation of illiquidity. Another situation that may arise is that the user of a cryptographic network is in a stage of losses in their business, until it reaches a point where it is not sustainable to manage and sustain their digital securities.

- Wallets

IN THE DIGITAL WORLD, given its ability to allow the cybernaut the possibility to create and innovate from the most elementary, it becomes evident a series of threats that put at risk and affect, among many; the financial sector, where cryptocurrencies are often very desirable, generating attacks and invasion of data in stores and virtual transactions.

THE MOST COMMON risks and threats that can even affect your secret digital wallet, would be:

- USING digital providers without prestige and proven guarantee in the network.

Forking digital platforms has become a favorite occupation for cyber attackers. When looking for a cryptographic service provider, you should try to verify that its domain corresponds to a secure and genuine website.

- SIMPLE PROTECTION of your identity

IT IS advisable to use passwords that really guarantee the protection of your identity, avoiding the use of pseudonyms and easily predictable codes: *PETER1234* .

.   .   .

- Do not back up wallets

It is advisable to make frequent updates to your digital wallet, using different means, resources and locations to keep them encrypted and thus keep a product as important as a wallet, safe and well protected.

- Do not encrypt the wallet The wallet encryption is crucial, especially when it is stored in an online network. As is to be expected and no matter how much attention we pay in establishing access keys and strong passwords, they will always be sensitive to violation. For this reason, it is advisable to use the DESlock+ tool to encrypt files containing any sensitive information.

- Use wallet only on mobile devices

Be careful! Particularly if you have to move large sums of money. A cell phone can be lost and crucial information can be lost along with important data that can be very vulnerable.

5

THE MOST EFFECTIVE WAY TO TRADE BITCOIN

Basic principles of cryptocurrency trading

L et us first define trading as the activity consisting in buying and selling of assets quoted on the network with high market liquidity represented in shares and currencies. This financial market is electronic and regulated. Its main objective is to obtain a profit and an economic benefit when the operation generates a capital gain.

Trading is a speculative type of operation and stock market activity, and is therefore radically subject to the ups and downs of the market. Its operations are based on buying an asset at the best price and then selling it at a higher and higher price or buying it back for a lower cost.

The following is a brief and basic description of ideas that traders should consider for better results. The statements apply in essence to the foreign exchange market and equally apply as general guidance for traders.

Having time

Avoid falling into the most common mistake made by traders due to impatience. Activating a position too quickly and in turn choosing a position size that is too large. Do not go fast.

Small trades

Keep relatively small positions. This will give excellent results in the face of high value offers or demands that cannot be predicted on the network.

Passive herd behavior

When a market phase is sustained long enough, the relationship between trend-following traders and mean reversion becomes increasingly one-sided. An attractive and interesting movement of great interaction is generated, demand increases, stocks rise and everyone wants to buy. Profits or losses can be made. However, many traders will continue to wait and remain patient until the last moment, so the moves will intensify towards the end of the day, when trend continuation indicators are considered more, especially on Fridays.

Keeping a reserve

Due to the market's great ability to maximize the spectrum, it is important to maintain a capital reserve. The optimal and recommended amount is 50% of the trading capital.

Taking profits

To make more money, it is just as important to generate profits as it is to limit losses. We should not be fooled by the apparent success and achievement of some individual positions. Profits must be made. It is necessary to establish a firm and feasible objective from the beginning and set or anchor it to achieve it.

Trading Risks and Profits (Long and Short Term Trading)

On the risk-reward ratio for trading, analysts converge on a much discussed and controversial topic, as while some traders claim that it is totally unproductive, others value it as the Holy Grail of e-commerce which should be part of every trading strategy.

In essence, the risk-to-reward ratio helps quantify the distance from entry to stop loss and from entry to take-profit order and then makes a comparison between the two distances. When the trader is well aware of the risk-reward ratio of his trades, he has the power to easily calculate the demanded profit rate. The trader can comfortably check whether the risk-to-reward ratio is large enough for his average profit rate or whether he should avoid a trade when the risk-to-reward ratio is too small.

We will often come across comments from traders who take for granted that the risk-to-reward ratio is useless, which could not be further from the truth. Although the risk-to-reward ratio alone is worthless, when used in combination with other trading metrics, it immediately becomes one of the most powerful trading tools.

Long-term trading strategies are those that tend to extend over a whole day or even several days. There are also longer-term strategies, but these are much less common in a market like Forex, which is determined by its great laboriousness when it comes to investing. A tactic that remains open from one day to the next is considered to be a long-term strategy in the foreign exchange market.

These strategies are not at all recommended for those who have just arrived on the platform, because making long term predictions requires a more precise and deeper fundamental analysis and a tech-nical study that takes into account more variables. It is therefore a strategy considered rather for people with a great knowledge of the market and a certain trajectory in the field of investors.

Long-term strategies do not need the constant attention of the investor and thanks to Forex orders it is possible to set a stop loss, limiting the losses that the operation could produce. While, as cons, we find the existence of a great "cold blood". There are operations so attractive and coveted, that the investor is reluctant to abandon them, especially if a fall in the price generates money losses, rather than profits.

To speak of short-term trading means, as the phrase itself indicates, to acquire and trade securities in a short period of time, even in the same day, hours or even minutes. If a user is not with this system, he could lose enough money. Therefore, it is advisable to know some strategies for short-term trading.

There are different guidelines that work very well to trade stocks in a short period of time. Below, we will share the simplest ones, in beginner mode. In this sense, it is important to handle a little bit of stock market terminology. Thus, we speak of going "long" in a transaction when we buy and then sell.

On the other hand, we enter "short" when we sell to then buy, the platform offers brokers that allow you to do this. It is also important to know that, for short-term trading, the ideal time to enter a security is when its price bounces. From then on, certain strategies can be applied.

- Buy assets at the moment they are at their lowest point, then they will start to rise.

- Open short, i.e.; sell when there is a downtrend in a security and resistance occurs.

-Long in countertrend when there is a downtrend, to buy a security when its price has overshot in the fall.

- Short in countertrend for a security that potentially its value.

- Iron technique, which consists of entering a security very carefully.

It is like when we do not know if the temperature of the iron is too high, we always take it with care. The same happens with a security, which we believe is trending upwards.

We invest in it from small amounts waiting for the perception of its rise to be fulfilled.

Where to trade.

The most secure ones: **Coinbase Pro, Binance, eToro**

Because it is an activity of buying and selling par excellence, with interesting detailed process of monitoring securities from the web, and given its global growth which is estimated at more than eight million traders approximately, there are platforms strictly designed to meet the operational needs of such an interesting and lucrative market, in which many lose, few others win.

Trading platforms are the best resource and indispensable support for those who venture and operate in the digital market world. These tools constitute a fundamental work support for any investor who is dedicated to the financial markets through the Internet.

It is a special software designed to support market analysis, to receive live prices of the necessary financial instruments available to invest and to open, control and close positions according to the decisions that the trader determines, and according to his stock funds.

Choosing the most convenient platform, the one that best suits your profile is basic to have success and excellent results in the operative management.

Online trading or what some define as speculating on the financial markets on the web, translates into taking advantage of changes and fluctuations in asset prices in order to make money, a crucial point; between buying and selling, it is already possible to sell a product that does not belong to you.

The online trading, in addition, is characterized by being a software accessible to anyone with a computer and internet access has the opportunity to enter the web. For those who are looking to start as a trader and begin to navigate this sea of cryptographic possibilities, the recommendation is to take your first steps guided by the hand supported by the knowledge and skills of a broker.

A broker is a financial entity or company in charge of executing buy and sell orders; for which it receives fees for its respective professional services. A broker or stockbroker, as they are also known, is licensed to buy and sell shares in the stock markets. Traders need a broker to operate in these markets themselves.

The main function that a financial broker must fulfill is to guarantee the correct functioning of the market, in addition to providing a comprehensive platform for traders, so that they can operate with the appropriate and safe guidelines through it.

Learning to trade in three simple steps:

- The strategies of those who obtain good results must be followed without doubts: This means that within any field in which we find ourselves, we must have our reservations of those who do not obtain results. For this reason, we must accept the advice of the experts and most knowledgeable in the field.

- Just as when a person goes to the gym to fulfill his routine training or is conditioned to climb a mountain, so a future trader or who already has experience, must instruct and apply what he has learned on this path, so he can assess the results from a first-person perspective.

- To begin with the use of low-risk profiles and limited capital so that in this way one acquires security, thus taking the first step without fear or trepidation, with the conviction that, in each transaction, something new will be learned.

Some of the most recommended trading platforms:

- NAGA:

Considered the most complete trading application.

- ProRealTime: Characteristic for being a multibroker platform.

- MetaTrader: Specialized for Forex investments.

- NinjaTrader: Platform that provides access to the futures and currency markets.

Trading with Coinbase Pro

In this context, trading through the Coinbase Pro platform is simple enough, and translates into the buying and selling of cryptocurrencies for the purpose of making profits. This means that in Coinbase Pro we can make exchanges of our fiat currency for cryptocurrencies or these for other pairs, such as Bitcoin for Ethereum or Litecoin for Bitcoin Cash, among many other options.

Coinbase Pro enjoys great prestige after having two types of operations that make it different from other platforms. If the operating system has limit and stop orders, as well as the charting system and indicators available.

Limit Order

Let's see a very practical example to understand the Coinbase Pro Limit order.

Let's suppose that the price of a cryptocurrency today is $200, however we are not willing to pay such amount of money and we believe that a good offer could be $180. For that reason we publish a limit order for 180$ and, in case the price falls to that figure, the purchase is done automatically and immediately.

In this way we have created an offer and at the same time we are looking for the possibility of finding a buyer. We have not simply bought at the market price as in a market order, we have created an offer.

The most relevant and major advantage of a limit order in Coinbase Pro, as we have mentioned before, is that it does not apply commissions or extra charges.

Stop Order

This is an ideal type of order to give us protection against unforeseen market movements. Thanks to this Coinbase Pro tool we can add a stop-loss through which our order is canceled once the value reaches that particular price.

Trading with Binance

In Binance Exchange we have at hand a technological platform for trading in which it is possible to operate with Bitcoin, other cryptocurrencies and their derivatives, with interfaces perfectly adaptable to each level of experience and demand as a trader. This portal also offers the alternative of making transactions and operations with leverage up to 10x.

With just the basic registration of an email address and without going through any identity verification process, you are already part of the Binance platform, which allows you to start the trading process after a maximum daily withdrawal limit of 2BTC.

Easy trading from the Binance platform is the well-known cryptocurrency exchange. In it, you only have to search and select the cryptocurrencies you wish to exchange and execute the transaction. Its operation is very similar to the exchange services found in Shape-

Shift or Changelly, except that the exchanges are made internally, within your Binance wallet.

To perform this trading modality, it is first necessary to have a balance in your Binance Spot wallet. Then you must select the trade button on the top menu, and from the drop-down list select the easy option.

Each cryptocurrency has a minimum and a maximum limit for easy trading. For Bitcoin it is 0.002BTC as minimum trade amount.

In the easy trading box you must choose the cryptocurrency to process and send along with the amount of the operation. On the other hand, you must place the cryptocurrency you want to receive in the box below. Once you have done all of the above, click on "Preview Conversion".

Before closing the easy trade operation, a confirmation box will appear on the screen with the details of the transaction.

From this small box, where the transaction must be confirmed, you will see the total amount that will be received in the selected cryptocurrency, together with the exchange rate. Inside the confirm button you will find a 30-second counter indicating that the exchange price will be frozen for that period of time. In case of not accepting, the process must be restarted. Likewise, upon confirmation, the exchange is performed immediately and the available balance in your wallet can be verified.

Trading with eToro

eToro is considered by the community to be the leading social trading platform on the web, offering an outstanding range of services to all its users and a wide range of cutting-edge financial instruments. Among its most outstanding features is "copy trading", which allows you to emulate the trades of other investors on the same platform. We would like to highlight this tool, which should be made known.

eToro's Copy Trader is eToro's most prominent and popular feature, which allows you to see what other traders are doing in real time and have the ability to copy their trades automatically. Copy

Trader also allows you to follow, share and contact any user or investor anywhere in the world, directly from the platform.

In addition to the above, Copy Trader allows those who are just starting out and learning the fundamentals of the markets to benefit from the experience of the best investors, copying them and instantly replicating their investments in their own portfolio.

Becoming a Copy Trader of other investors does not generate any extra charges or commissions for management fees or any other additional charges for the user. Since, just by belonging to the program and being copied, these investors obtain their earnings as Popular Investor. The minimum amount to Copy Trader another investor is $200- eToro's Copy Trading is not just copying trades that other investors have made, it is a whole environment in a collaborative community of short- and long-term investors, where it is possible to interact, share and learn. With optimal use of this tool and proper management, you can view millions of portfolios, statistics, risk ratings, and even more from other traders within eToro.

6

BITCOIN MAXIMALISTS AND WHY YOU SHOULD LISTEN TO THEM

An influencer is a personality that enjoys a certain level of popularity, credibility and sympathy through social networks, becoming their own product, topic or highlighting another in particular, either brand or service; among other qualities references more.

Today, social networks have triggered an endless number of talents, events, facts, personalities, etc. showing us and letting us know the world as never before, as it is, live and in real time regardless of time and distance. The networks are an unstoppable boom of information, recreation and education that are ready and available every second.

And when it comes to talents, known people and products, there is one sector that has a huge menu of alternatives on the net, and that is none other than the financial sector. We will dedicate this chapter to make known or remember, as the case may be, two figures who enjoy the admiration of the community that follows them and who have shared their talks and presentations online or in person. We refer to Sunny Decree (Switzerland) and Davinciji5 (Chile).

Davinciji5

VLOGGER WITH HIS youtube channel based in Chile.

DEDICATED to technical analysis on Bitcoin, Ethereum and cryptos.

ON HIS YOUTUBE CHANNEL, he talks about how to earn through cryptocurrency business.

Davinciji5 believes that Bitcoin will free humanity from debt slavery.

HE BELIEVES that Bitcoin will be the fair and honest money of the future.

A programmer and web content generator who since 2011 has been preaching that Bitcoin is the money of the future and that the way it is structured makes it the safest way to protect your money, he estimates, that we will see the value of Bitcoin at least $100,000 by 2021 and that we will witness the largest transfer of wealth we have ever seen.

HE BROADCASTS his videos in English and Spanish with subtitles.

· · ·

HIS SOCIAL NETWORKS:

INSTAGRAM: @davinciji15
 - Followers: 10.9k

TWITTER: @pandoraswallet_
 - Followers: 4,571

YOUTUBE: Dvinciji15
 - Subscribers: 186,000

PandorasWallet.com

STATUS: Active

SUNNY DECREE

VLOGGER WITH HIS youtube channel based in Switzerland.

MAIN SUBJECT MATTER based on the digital crypto market.

FINANCIAL ANALYST BASED ON BITCOIN.

· · ·

TECHNICAL ECONOMIC ANALYSIS with guidance suitable for cryptocurrency beginners, and especially inclined towards Bitcoin and experienced leverage traders.

The emphasis of his publications is on technical analysis of digital currency and cryptocurrency price prediction.

CONTENT GENERATOR through his digital Youtube channel.

HE BROADCASTS his videos in English and German, although his channel is more English-oriented.

HIS SOCIAL NETWORKS:

INSTAGRAM: @sunnydecree.official
   - Followers: 10.4k

TWITTER: @sunnydecree
   - Followers: 44.4k

YOUTUBE: sunny decree
   - Subscribers: 151,000

LINKEDIN: Sunny Decree
   - + of 500 contacts

STATUS: Active

.   .   .

By December 2019 the digital platform YouTube deleted a significant number of its videos to the point that it has suspended live transmissions related to the topic of cryptoassets, claiming that it was due to failures originated in the logarithms of the operating system of the channel. This event caught the attention of the media and within three days its channel and services were reinstated. Currently, Sunny Decree maintains its virtual channel in operation.

The recent importance that Influencers have given to digital marketing has provided a boost and prestige to goods, products and services that are promoted, used and consumed by these figures of social networks. Today, these networks play an innovative role in the dissemination of messages that invite us to take a certain position on a message that seeks to positively impact society through applications that constantly travel in our hands.

Influencers in the current stage of digital marketing are opinion leaders in the world of new technologies; they are common people or recognized figures who have developed a very good reputation in their social networks, blogs and websites; even in the new and practical instant messaging systems, as they share with their community and followers their experiences, experiences and knowledge on a particular topic, on which they practically become gurus for their thousands of fans.

We already use the term Influencers more frequently and little by little the different generations are adapting to this new communication trend. You may have heard of them, who we call them as bloggers, youtubers and even instagramers, but, ultimately, we can call them all the same thing: Influencers.

7

MAKING PASSIVE INCOME WITH BITCOIN AND OTHER CRYPTOCURRENCIES

A s you may have noticed throughout the development of the book, there are currently several ways to generate money with cryptocurrencies, there are many opportunities. While there are some that are riskier (and depend on your ability) such as trading, DeFi platforms, etc, there are others that are more recommended and less risky, such as making Hodl of a cryptocurrency and wait for its price to rise, although this earning model is absolutely passive, as it is a long-term strategy, we have other strategies that can also help you generate passive income, as is the strategy that I will present below.

This strategy has existed for many years, is widely used by banks today, although in a higher percentage of profit, this generates interest with your assets.

In the world of cryptocurrencies this modality already exists and is led by one of the most reliable companies in the environment: BlockFi, which is backed by the Gemini exchange and people as recognized in the environment as Anthony Pompliano.

BlockFi allows us to transfer our funds to the platform and generate an annual interest that goes from 6% (for cryptocurrencies such as Bitcoin) or almost 10% with stablecoins (which are cryptocurrencies that are 1 to 1 with the dollar, such as USDT and USDC to name a few).

IF YOU ARE interested in this modality, you can open a BlockFi account at the following link and earn $250 of Bitcoin for free:

GET your BONUS on BlockFi here

IN CASE you are reading this book in the printed version you can scan the following QR code with your cell phone:

8

THE MOST IMPORTANT THINGS TO KEEP IN MIND WITH BITCOIN

To conclude this book, I would like to thank you for taking the time to read it, I wanted to clarify a few things before finishing.

Many people have tried dabbling in cryptocurrencies, some with success others with moderate results, but all with results in the end, the important thing is that you keep in mind that the cryptocurrency market is a highly manipulated market, which is why I recommend that you always pay attention to the indicators that you can see in TradingView, see the signals it sends you, continue learning about trading, if you are interested you can dedicate yourself to them, but if not you can dedicate yourself to do HODL (the meaning of this within the Cryptocurrencies is related to buy coins when there is a significant decline (for example if Bitcoin is at $58000 and falls to $36500 there is where you buy and go buying as it falls, never when it goes up, this is known as Dollar Cost Averaging is a strategy widely used in the trading environment) and keep those cryptocurrencies for years until they double, triple or quadruple their value, it is not uncommon in the environment, as well have done those early adopters who bought Bitcoin when it was worth $0.006 cents, did HODL for 14 years and when Bitcoin reached its all-time high of $20,000 dollars in 2017 and $60,000 in 2021, sold everything and became millionaires. But as always, choose the method you like best and follow it at your own risk.

FINALLY, I would like to know your comments to continue to nurture this book and to help many more people, for them would you help us by leaving a review of this book, in order to continue providing great books to you, my readers, which I appreciate very much.

LINKS for you
Check crypto prices here:
https://coinmarketcap.com/
Get free Bitcoin:
Get free bitcoin here
Get your BlockFi bonus here:
https://blockfi.com/?ref=76971ae9

Trading crypto:

Binance

Bitmex

Buy Crypto:

Coinbase

CEX.IO

Changally

Localbitcoins

Donde guardar tus criptomonedas:

Get the Trezor Model T here

Get the Trezor Model ONE here

Get a Ledger Nano S here

More trading tools at:

www.TradingView.com

www.ingramcontent.com/pod-product-compliance
Lightning Source LLC
Chambersburg PA
CBHW030524210326
41597CB00013B/1016